MICHAEL CHIARELLO'S
CASUAL COOKING

MICHAEL CHIARELLO'S CASUAL COOKING

wine country recipes for family and friends—a napastyle cookbook

MICHAEL CHIARELLO WITH JANET FLETCHER | PHOTOGRAPHS BY DEBORAH JONES

CHRONICLE BOOKS

SAN FRANCISCO

Library of Congress Cataloging-in-Publication Data available.

ISBN 0-8118-3383-6

Manufactured in China

Prop styling by Sara Slavin

Food styling by Sandra Cook

Designed by Level, Calistoga, CA

Distributed in Canada by Raincoast Books

9050 Shaughnessy Street

Vancouver, BC V6P 6E5

10 9 8 7 6 5 4 3 2 1

Chronicle Books LLC

85 Second Street

San Francisco, California 94105

www.chroniclebooks.com

To home cooks who understand that gathering friends and family around the table is the best way to celebrate life.

To EG: the greatest gift of all. *Ti amerò sempre*.

To Margaux, Felicia, and Giana: my daughters, my heart, my life.

LEFT: *SALSA DI PARMIGIANO*, PAGE 45;

CENTER: CHOCOLATE ESPRESSO GELATO, PAGE 207

My home is in the Napa Valley, America's Tuscany. Like that famous Italian wine region, the valley is blessed with a Mediterranean climate, which is reflected in a landscape of leafy grapevines and shimmering olive trees. People live close to the ground here, their lives attuned to the seasonal rhythms of the wine grape, their gardens yielding fruits and vegetables year-round.

Like Tuscans, my Napa Valley neighbors take profound pleasure in daily life. Almost everyone lives here because they choose to, because they want to be part of a small, picturesque community dominated by agriculture. They cook with enthusiasm and eat with relish, and they love nothing better than sharing the wine in their cellars. Cooking for friends is a favorite pastime, and no one is in a hurry to get up from the table.

Casual cooking in Napa Valley means working in sync with the seasons and celebrating whatever the market brings. It means simplifying dishes to let good ingredients speak for themselves. And because most of my Napa Valley friends are as busy as anyone in a big-city job, it means making the most of limited kitchen time.

After twenty-five years as a professional cook, I've developed a number of techniques for getting the flavor I want in the time I have. Anyone can learn to cook well, but learning to cook smart can take years. With this book, I want to share not only a valued collection of recipes but also my thoughts on how to provision your kitchen so that you have a running start on great meals.

I also want to share a way of thinking about cooking that I hope will enrich that daily activity for you. We experience food not just with our palates, but with all our senses. We taste first with our eyes, embracing the colors and shapes of a dish and imagining the flavors to follow. We savor the aromas of a chicken roasted with rosemary before we sample it. We notice texture, the contrast of crunchy and creamy, or hard and soft. We hear a steak sizzle in a skillet and our appetite is aroused.

If a dish has history or deep cultural meaning, we also taste intellectually. And I believe we taste with our hearts when we receive the gift of someone's cooking. I want to encourage you to engage all your conventional senses in cooking, but I especially hope you will engage your emotional side.

When I prepare certain family recipes or use my mother's old food mill, I'm reminded of earlier times and of long-gone loved ones. Cooking for friends and family now allows me to celebrate their presence and helps keep them close to me. Shared food creates shared memories. To me, times spent in the kitchen and at the table with others are among the most meaningful moments in life.

Hundreds of cookbooks can tell you how to get through a Saturday-night dinner party. This book is for the rest of your life, for family meals and simple gatherings where fussed-over food wouldn't fit. Now that I'm no longer responsible for the daily production of a busy restaurant, I'm reveling in the pleasures of cooking at home. The following recipes are the ones that friends and family have most enjoyed at my table.

You'll notice that I spend a lot of time encouraging you and advising you on how to set up a pantry. To me, this is a large part of cooking smart. You invest a little front-end time, but it pays off hugely down the road. Supermarkets are filled with convenience foods, but most of those products don't deliver quality and many aren't wholesome. I believe in stocking a pantry (and refrigerator and freezer) with convenience foods, but with foods that enhance your cooking, not with those that replace it.

As you'll see, my concept of the pantry also encompasses a number of homemade items that lay the foundation for innumerable quick meals. Italian cooking has always been a cuisine of preservation, and some of these preparations, like Calabrese Antipasto (page 49), are foods I knew as a child. Making them for your pantry can be an excuse to bring friends and family together. You share the work and share the results, and create a memory of an enjoyable day in the process.

With your pantry in place, you're ready to cook from this book. I hope you'll enjoy preparing and eating these dishes as much as I've enjoyed recording them for you.

pantry

When I take my three daughters to visit their Italian cousins in the mountains of Northern California, we spend an enormous amount of time around the table. The minute we arrive, the cousins bring out the pecorino, the salamis, the oil-cured olives, and bread, and we have a simple and delicious Italian lunch. At dinnertime, out come the pickled vegetables for antipasto, good imported pasta, and jars of last summer's homemade tomato sauce. Morning, noon, and night, their meals are easy because the pantry is full—full of great Mediterranean

ingredients and preserved foods that they have bought (like the salamis and cheeses) or made (like the pickles and sauces) at peak season.

My relatives don't cook from recipes; they cook from what they have. Oil-packed Italian tuna becomes the centerpiece of a salad with garden tomatoes and cucumbers, or the inspiration for a quick pasta sauce or a smooth mousse for crostini. Polenta from the pantry becomes a soft, creamy foundation for greens; leftover, it becomes a layered "lasagne" the following day.

This is the resourceful cooking I grew up with—cooking based on a full larder that gives you a head start when it's time to make dinner. My mother cooked this way, preserving the fleeting harvest from our garden for enjoyment later. Now I cook this way, too, at my home in Napa Valley, although I have expanded my pantry in directions my mother never imagined. (I guarantee there was no basil oil in the house when I was growing up.)

What follows is a guide to some of the pantry items that I keep on hand. Some are store bought, some home-made. All of them, if purchased or made with care, will make your cooking easier, tastier, and more satisfying.

STORE-BOUGHT PANTRY—Your cooking can be helped or hindered by your raw materials, and that's as true for pantry items as it is for produce, meats, and fish. It may seem frugal to buy inexpensive mass-market brands of olive oil, vinegar, tuna, and anchovies, but that's a false economy. Even if you follow recipes religiously, dishes won't taste right, and you will have wasted your time and money.

Over the years, I've developed preferences and prejudices regarding commercial pantry staples. Supermarkets are filled with all kinds of packaged foods, but I urge you to seek out those made with care and integrity. The better and broader your pantry, the easier it is to make great quick meals.

Before you start filling your pantry with any of the following items, do some spring cleaning. If you haven't cooked with a product in six months or a year, give it away; you will probably never use it and someone else might. Rebuild your pantry selectively, with quality ingredients, and don't forget to collect tastes from places you travel. What follows are my pantry selections, but your own pantry should reflect how you like to cook, eat, and live.

ANCHOVIES—I prefer salt-packed to oil-packed anchovies. Salt-packed anchovies tend to be meatier and more flavorful, and I can dress them with the high-quality olive oil of my choosing. Many oil-packed brands use inferior olive oil or soybean oil.

Salt-packed anchovies are whole fish, but they are easy to fillet. Just hold them under cold running water and use your fingers to tease the two fillets apart down the back. The skeleton will lift out easily. Rinse the fillets well and pat dry. Refrigerate unused salt-packed anchovies in their tin, tightly covered.

If you are buying anchovy fillets in oil, look for those packed in olive oil. Some are sold in glass jars, so you can see how fat and meaty the fillets are. Rather than using the oil from the tin or jar in your dish, use fresh extra-virgin olive oil. If the anchovies are in a tin and you don't use them all, transfer the extra fillets to a nonreactive container, cover with good olive oil and a lid, and refrigerate. If the unused anchovies are in a jar, simply top up the jar with good olive oil so the fillets are protected from air and refrigerate.

BEANS—Dried beans are a produce item like green beans or asparagus; they just happen to be dried. You should choose them with the same care you take in choosing any fresh vegetable. Buy them from a market that turns its stock over frequently so you can be sure the beans are no more than a year old. After a year, many beans get so dry that they won't rehydrate properly.

The best place to buy dried beans is at a farmers' market or specialty-produce market that offers more unusual heirloom varieties. You'll find the best selection and quality in the fall, when the beans are freshly dried. Look for cannellini beans, borlotti beans (a type of cranberry bean that Italians love for soup), or the giant white Greek *gigandes*.

At home, store beans in an airtight container away from heat. Date them and use them within a year, or replace them.

Canned beans are not a favorite of mine with one exception. I think chickpeas (*ceci* in Italian) survive the canning process well, and I often use them, well rinsed, in soups, salads, and antipasti, such as *Ceci alla Siciliana* (page 48).

BREAD — Good bread is a staple of life for me, as essential to daily contentment as wine. In my kitchen, I observe its cycle of life and try to use it well at every stage, which to me is the essence of good cooking. Of course, fresh bread is essential for soaking up sauces, for serving with sweet butter and prosciutto, and for making great sandwiches from Forever-Roasted Pork with Toasted Spice Rub (page 161). When the bread is a day or two old, I'll use it for *Panzanella* Croutons (page 38), Parmesan Toasts (page 84) or *bruschetta*. And when it gets really stale, I'll grind it very fine for bread crumbs (page 38), a kitchen essential for coating Veal Milanese (page 155) or making stuffed baked clams (page 57).

Throughout this book, I've called for loaves that are "country style," meaning that they contain nothing but flour, water, yeast, and salt. They should have a good, sturdy crust and a reasonably dense, chewy interior. Many communities now have artisan bakers making these specialty breads, so you can avoid airy, flavorless supermarket loaves. Good bread does cost more, but it's well worth it to get a preservative-free product that has texture, flavor, and soul. Please don't put it in a plastic bag, which ruins the crust. If you can't eat it before it goes stale, it would be better to freeze it.

CAPERS — Capers are flower buds from the caper plant (*Capparis spinosa*). My favorite capers are salt-packed and come from the Italian island of Pantelleria, near Sicily. The salt seems to preserve their pure flavor and bouquet better than a brine does. Salt-packed capers should be stored in the salt in which they were originally packed and then rinsed just before using. Brined capers should also be rinsed before using, unless the dish can use some of that briny flavor. Capers are almost always chopped before using.

You may also find caper berries at the market. These are, literally, the fruit of the caper plant, containing the seeds capable of reproducing a new plant. They are usually sold brined with the stems attached, although you may find salt-packed ones. They may be as small as a caper or as large as an olive. They're great in a martini, as a garnish for sliced cured meats, or in any dish that calls for capers.

CHEESE — I keep several aged cheeses in my refrigerator at all times, for cooking and for impromptu nibbling.

I always have Parmigiano Reggiano on hand for pasta. Be sure the wheel your piece comes from has those two words— Parmigiano Reggiano—stamped on the rind, your guarantee of authenticity. Although people think of Parmesan as just a grating cheese, it's a wonderful table cheese, too. Bring it to room temperature and serve it with a table knife so people can break off chunks, rather than slice it. With a few drops of *aceto balsamico tradizionale,* it's heaven. Notice the crystalline texture and the orange-peel flavor as the nuggets of cheese dissolve on your tongue.

I usually have grana padano around, too. It's similar to Parmigiano Reggiano but not as aged, and it's less expensive. I often use it with seafood.

I grew up with pecorino romano, the sharp, salty, aged sheep's milk cheese from southern Italy. I like it on bean and vegetable soups and on vegetable pastas, but you may find it a little too sharp. Often I'll mix equal parts of grated Parmesan and pecorino for passing at the table with soup or pasta.

Vella Dry Jack from Sonoma, California, is another personal favorite. This golden, nutty, aged cow's milk cheese is delicious before dinner with salami and sliced fennel, or after dinner with nuts and pears. During World War I, which disrupted shipments of Parmigiano Reggiano from Italy, the Italian-American community used aged Dry Jack for grating. It's still a great choice if you find a well-aged wheel.

I prefer not to store cheese in plastic wrap, which smothers it and imparts an unpleasant taste. Instead, I recommend wrapping it in butcher paper or in aluminum foil. If you're not going to use it soon, put the wrapped cheese inside a lidded plastic container.

I also use a lot of goat cheese, ricotta, mozzarella, and mascarpone in my cooking, but these cheeses are highly perishable, so I buy them only as needed.

Nonfat cheeses don't make any sense to me. If you're trying to keep your fat intake down, buy better cheese, not worse cheese. You'll be satisfied with less of it.

CHOCOLATE — Your dessert making will benefit if you buy premium chocolate. It costs more, but you are paying for better-quality beans and more careful processing. I have come to be fond of Scharffen Berger (see Resources, page 210), a relatively new chocolate made in California, and I am particularly partial to the bittersweet. Its richness is incredible, and the winy taste lingers a long time in your mouth. Sometimes, for dessert, I'll put out a few roasted nuts and a plate of small chunks of bittersweet chocolate. People will sit for hours, nibbling and savoring that luscious chocolate.

Keep chocolate well wrapped in a cool, dark, dry place.

MUSHROOMS — Dried mushrooms are a powerful flavoring agent themselves, not a substitute for fresh mushrooms. I always have dried porcini (*Boletus edulis*) on hand, and I make sure they're from Italy. Those from South America are less expensive but not nearly as good. Reconstituted in water, porcini add a woodsy, earthy character and depth of flavor to soups and sauces, like my veal and pork bolognese (page 102).

Soften dried porcini in warm water for about 30 minutes. Don't try to speed things up with hot water, which would compromise the flavor. Also, use only as much water as you need to cover the mushrooms so that you don't dilute the flavor of the soaking water, which you should always use. Porcini can be gritty. Always lift them out of the soaking water, leaving any grit behind, then strain the flavorful water through cheesecloth or paper towels and add it to your sauce or stew.

Store porcini in an airtight container in a cool place.

MUSTARD — Dijon mustard is the energizer and emulsifier in many of my salad dressings. It has a depth of flavor that goes beyond merely hot. In fact, mustard isn't hot until the milled mustard seed is combined with vinegar. I use only French Dijon mustard, made by blending the milled seed of the mustard plant with, typically, white wine vinegar. It does lose its pungency over time, so if your jar has been in the refrigerator for a while, taste the mustard to make sure it still has punch. Ballpark mustard is fine on a burger or hot dog, but it's not a good choice for serious cooking.

OLIVE OIL — Flavorful olive oil is the healthful foundation of my cooking and of any Mediterranean kitchen. Even though, at any one time, I may have bottles from several different producers in my pantry, they all fall into one of three categories.

Pure olive oil is what I use for frying, for making flavored oils, for mayonnaise, and for some traditional Italian pastries. After olives are cold-pressed to make extra-virgin olive oil, processors use heat and sometimes chemicals to extract yet more oil. This is pure olive oil. When it's first made, it has almost no flavor, color, or aroma, so a little extra-virgin olive oil is typically added back. Pure olive oil can be heated to a higher temperature without smoking than extra-virgin oil, so it's a good choice for deep-frying. In stores, look for oil that is simply labeled "olive oil." When my recipes specify olive oil as opposed to extra-virgin olive oil, this is the type I mean.

My everyday extra-virgin olive oil is a relatively inexpensive oil that I use freely and liberally in cooked and uncooked dishes. I've never bought into the idea that you shouldn't cook with extra-virgin olive oil. It does lose some of its aroma and flavor when exposed to heat, but it adds a richness and depth to food that would be lacking if you made the same dish with pure olive oil. Taste the moderately priced brands available to you and find one that you like. Buying by the jug or gallon may save you money, and the oil will last for at least a year in a cool, dark place.

My best, priciest extra-virgin olive oil is reserved for use as a condiment, drizzled on dishes off the heat to preserve its aroma and flavor. This is the oil I drizzle on a thick grilled steak, on white beans (page 144), or on charcoal-grilled garlic-rubbed toast. You'll find great extra-virgin oils these days from Italy, France, Spain, Greece, and even California. We Californians are very proud of our fledgling olive oil producers—I've been involved for many years, with my own label—and I encourage you to support this domestic cottage industry.

When you get to know olive oils, you can make finer distinctions among them. Early-harvest oils tend to be greener, more pungent, and peppery. That's the style of oil I would choose for drizzling on white beans or a steak. Late-harvest oils are usually more straw colored, delicate, and fruity; they're a good choice for seafood and other mild dishes.

Store olive oil away from light and heat. For convenience, you may want to keep a small amount near the stove, but put it in a lightproof container and as far from the heat as your arm can reach.

OLIVES—Good olives for the kitchen and table are not those black things you used to put on your fingers as a kid. (Those are canned ripe olives, and they've been so overprocessed, they have no flavor.) My favorite olives are Greek Kalamata, an almond-shaped, brine-cured ripe olive; Italian Gaeta, a rounder, brine-cured ripe olive; French Picholine, a mild brine-cured green olive with pointed ends; and the wrinkled, dry-cured (also called oil-cured) olives that come from all over the Mediterranean. Sometimes I'll warm these dry-cured olives with olive oil, a bay leaf or sprig of thyme, some red pepper flakes and a strip of lemon or orange zest and serve them warm with cocktails.

I prefer to buy olives with pits, because the pit helps the olive preserve its flavor and texture. Besides, part of the pleasure of eating an olive is nibbling around the pit. Most olives can be pitted easily by hand, but if they're stuck to the pit, just smash the flesh lightly with a cleaver first.

Store olives in the refrigerator, but bring them to room temperature before using.

PASTA—For a pasta lover like myself, the flavor and texture of the pasta is as important as what you put on it. Good pasta holds a sauce well; the sauce doesn't slip off. It also tastes of wheat and has "chew" to it. Lower-quality pasta is bland and slick and quickly goes from undercooked to soggy. Sauces don't cling to it, and there's no satisfaction in eating it.

You can buy inexpensive supermarket brands, or you can spend about twenty-five cents more a person and buy pasta of real quality. Look for Italian brands from artisan producers, such as Rustichella d'Abruzzo. De Cecco, a large but top-quality Italian producer, is a good value. Both brands put their pasta dough through bronze dies instead of through Teflon-coated ones to make the shapes. The bronze dies produce a rough texture that sauces cling to. (You can see this under a magnifying lens.) These brands also dry the pasta very slowly, which gives it a more uniform and pleasing texture when cooked.

I stock a lot of different shapes in my pantry, and they are not all interchangeable. Long noodles like spaghetti, spaghettini, and linguine are great for seafood sauces. For chunky sauces, I'll use a short pasta like penne or rigatoni. For tomato sauces, almost anything goes, so it's fun to play around with more unusual shapes like *gemelli* (twins) or *bucatini* (thick hollow spaghetti). Soup pasta, like *riso*, *ditalini*, and *acini di pepe*, is meant for floating in broth, although I also use *acini di pepe* for making pasta "risotto" (page 114).

PEPERONCINI—A hint of chili pepper (*peperoncino*) underlies a lot of my cooking, and I keep a couple of different kinds on hand. I use red pepper flakes often because they contribute a fundamental piquant flavor to Italian dishes that black pepper doesn't duplicate. Red pepper flakes need to be warmed in oil to release their heat and fragrance.

If I could have only one variety of chili pepper, I would choose the Calabrian chili (see Resources, page 210), which is fortunately available in some food shops carrying Italian products. The tiny, whole, brined red chilies have layers of fruity flavor and an almost smoky undertone. Minced fine, they add a complex and compelling warmth to tomato sauces and simmered dishes.

POLENTA—I've noticed a significant difference among polentas in how finely they are ground. Italian brands tend to be finer than American ones, and the fine polenta cooks up smoother. I prefer the imported product for all polenta recipes.

Like all ground grains (polenta is ground dried corn), polenta does not have an infinite shelf life. Keep it in a cool place, even in the refrigerator, to prolong its life, but you should probably replace any package that has been open more than a year.

RICE—For risotto and rice salads, I stock two short-grain rices: Arborio and Vialone Nano. A lot of the Arborio I use is California-grown; the Vialone Nano is from Italy. I tend to reach mostly for the Arborio, except when I'm doing an unadorned Risotto Bianco (page 121) or simple risotto milanese (risotto flavored with saffron). Then I'll use Vialone Nano because you can better appreciate its large, plump grains.

Keep rice in a cool, dry place.

SALT — If you change only one thing in your kitchen, make it the salt. You use it in almost everything you cook; upgrade your salt and the quality of your food will improve substantially.

I use gray salt from France's Brittany coast almost exclusively. It has a richness of flavor that makes my dishes appreciably better. It is minimally processed, so it contains all the minerals and micronutrients present in the salt naturally. Nothing needs to be added back, as it is for most table salt, because it was never taken out. When I started using gray salt, my craving for high-salt foods like potato chips vanished.

Most table salt has agents added to prevent caking, and I think you can taste them. Table salt is harsh; sea salt is mild and briny. I know that good sea salt is expensive, but you will find that it allows you to make your cooking much simpler. A sliced ripe tomato with extra-virgin olive oil and gray salt is satisfying all by itself.

Gray salt is moist and coarse and hard to distribute evenly. To make it easier to use for everyday seasoning, I dry large quantities of it in a 200°F oven for 2 hours, then pound it or grind it in a spice grinder until medium-coarse. I keep a big tin of it by my stove.

SALUMI — Italian-style cured meats—salami, mortadella, prosciutto, and the like—are almost always in my refrigerator because they make such easy antipasti. I'll put them out with bread sticks, olives, and some marinated chickpeas (page 48), sliced fennel, or radishes, and I've got a colorful and wine-friendly first course.

If you live in a town with an Italian-style delicatessen, you should have many choices of cured meats, like *soppressata* and *finocchiona*. Ask to taste before you buy, and you'll eventually develop favorites. An assortment arranged on a platter is always appetizing. The meats all tend to dry out quickly after slicing, so for longer keeping, buy a whole sausage or salami and slice it yourself.

TOMATOES — I keep canned whole tomatoes in my pantry and use them whenever I can't get fresh, ripe plum (Roma) tomatoes. I rarely buy canned diced tomatoes because it's so easy to dice them myself, and I almost never use tomato paste. The one canned tomato product I never buy is tomato puree, which is usually reconstituted tomato paste. If I need tomato puree, I'll puree the toma-toes in a blender or food mill myself, using canned whole tomatoes in winter, or peeled and seeded plum tomatoes in summer. It takes about 1½ pounds of fresh plum tomatoes to make 2 cups puree. A 28-ounce can of whole tomatoes makes about 3½ cups puree.

I'm a big fan of Muir Glen's organic canned tomato products. The company packs the tomatoes in an enameled rather than an unlined tin, so you don't get any off flavors.

TUNA — Imported oil-packed tuna is a pantry staple for me. I'll mix it with cooked white beans (page 125) or marinated chickpeas (page 48) to make a quick lunch or supper. I also use canned tuna for a speedy appetizer, *Spuma di Tonno* (page 45), that my guests always love. I recommend Italian or Portuguese tuna packed in olive oil. It's meaty and flavorful and a world apart from the water-packed white-meat tuna that most people buy.

VINEGAR — If you lined up a half-dozen different red wine vinegars from the supermarket, you might be surprised at the quality differences. Bad wine vinegar is harsh on the tongue, with an unpleasantly sharp aroma. Good wine vinegar is fruity and mellow and pleasant to smell. Even if it costs a bit more, I urge you to buy high-quality vinegar. Invest in several brands, then taste and compare. The wrong wine vinegar can ruin a salad. I particularly like the mild taste of Champagne vinegar, which I use whenever a dish requires white wine vinegar. Wine vinegars do oxidize and deteriorate with time. Buy small bottles and always smell the vinegar before you use it.

Of course, balsamic vinegar is an essential in my Italian-American kitchen. I keep a very fine, thick, aged aceto *balsamico tradizionale* for sprinkling sparingly on Parmesan cheese or on a grilled steak. I also keep a moderately priced, younger *balsamico* that I can use more freely in dishes like Italian Home-Style Onion Soup (page 78). Beware of inexpensive balsamic vinegars; some of them are little more than wine vinegar and caramel, and they won't give you the desired flavor.

HOMEMADE PANTRY—My own pantry contains a number of homemade "go-to" items: foundation ingredients, seasonings, and condiments that I turn to constantly and couldn't cook without. Some are family heirlooms, like My Mother's Tomato Sauce (page 32) and Damn Hot Peppers (page 37). Others are signature seasonings I've developed over the years, like Fennel Spice (page 23) and Prosciutto Bits (page 25).

I'm a big believer in taking some weekend time to make these helping-hand foods. Having them in the freezer, refrigerator, or pantry makes me feel secure, like having money in the bank. If you've got Peck Seasoning (page 25) and some thick pork chops, you've got the makings for a great dinner (page 160). I also use many of these pantry items as gifts.

Why not invite friends over and make some of these recipes together, then divide the results? The work will go faster, and when you use the items, you'll remember the pleasure and friendship of that day.

SPICED CANDIED WALNUTS—This is a method I learned from Cindy Pawlcyn, the Napa Valley chef. Make a lot so you have some to give away. The nuts are great to eat out of hand with a glass of Champagne, but they also have many other uses. Serve them with a cheese course, or stuff a fig with mascarpone and a candied walnut. They're also great on fall salads, such as the frisée, pear, and blue cheese salad on page 86.

Peanut or canola oil
1 teaspoon salt
½ teaspoon ground cinnamon
½ teaspoon cayenne pepper
¼ teaspoon freshly ground black pepper
4 cups walnut halves
1 cup confectioners' sugar, sifted

In a deep saucepan, pour oil to a depth of at least 3 inches and heat to 350°F. While the oil is heating, bring a large pot of water to a boil. Measure the salt, cinnamon, cayenne pepper, and black pepper into a small bowl and mix well. Holding the nuts in a sieve, dip them briefly into the boiling water, about 1 minute for large halves. Transfer to a large bowl with a little water clinging to them. (Blanching removes some of the tannins and makes walnuts taste sweet.) While the nuts are still hot and wet, add the sugar and toss well to coat evenly. The sugar will melt on contact with the hot nuts. Keep stirring and tossing until all the sugar has melted. If bits of unmelted sugar remain on the nuts, they will not fry properly.

Stir the nuts again before frying. Using a large slotted spoon, transfer a few nuts to the hot oil, allowing the foam to subside before adding another spoonful. (Otherwise, the oil could foam over and burn you.) Fry in small batches until the nuts are medium-brown, about 1 minute. Be careful not to overcook. Scatter on an unlined baking sheet to cool slightly.

While the nuts are still warm, transfer them to a bowl and sprinkle evenly with about half of the spice mix. Toss well to distribute the spices and then taste a nut. Add more spice mix to taste and toss well after each addition. When cool, pack in an airtight jar. They will keep at room temperature for at least 2 weeks.

MAKES ABOUT 4 CUPS

CHICKEN STOCK — Having homemade chicken stock in the freezer makes me feel like I'm ready for anything. With just a few vegetables, a little pasta, and some herbs snipped from the garden, I can make a pot of soup for dinner in minutes.

Cooking up a big batch of stock is a great rainy-day activity and one that will leave you with a sense of accomplishment. It takes only a few minutes to prepare the ingredients, then the stove does the rest. You only need to glance at the pot occasionally and skim the surface of the stock as necessary.

I use 5 pounds of chicken to yield about 1 gallon of stock. You can scale the recipe up or down, as you like.

2 pounds chicken thighs, skinned, or chicken legs
2 pounds chicken necks and backs
1 pound chicken wings, each wing cut into 3 pieces
2 onions, quartered
1 large carrot, peeled and halved
1 large celery rib, halved
1 cup roughly chopped fresh mushrooms
Stems from ½ bunch fresh Italian (flat-leaf) parsley
1 tablespoon black peppercorns
4 bay leaves, crumbled
6 quarts water

Rinse the chicken parts well. Put all the ingredients in a large stockpot. Bring to a simmer over moderate heat, skimming any foam that collects on the surface. Adjust the heat to maintain a bare simmer and cook uncovered for 3 to 4 hours, skimming as needed. Cool, then strain and refrigerate for up to 5 days or freeze for longer keeping. Before using, lift off and discard any congealed fat on the surface.

MAKES ABOUT 4 QUARTS

Michael's Notes: I use only parsley stems, not leaves, in stock. The leaves can give your stock a faint green cast.

CHEATER'S CHICKEN STOCK — Sometimes I reach into the freezer for homemade stock and come up empty-handed. When that happens, I head to the pantry for canned chicken broth, which I doctor with fresh vegetables and seasonings to give it a homemade taste.

2 cans (14½ ounces each) low-sodium chicken broth plus 1½ cans water
1 small celery rib, cut on the diagonal into 1-inch pieces
1 small carrot, peeled and cut on the diagonal into 1-inch pieces
½ cup roughly chopped fresh mushrooms
1 bay leaf, crumbled
¼ teaspoon black peppercorns
Stems from ¼ bunch fresh Italian (flat-leaf) parsley

Combine all the ingredients in a saucepan. Bring to a simmer over moderate heat, adjust the heat to maintain a gentle simmer, and cook for 30 minutes. Cool briefly, then strain. Use immediately, or refrigerate for up to 5 days.

MAKES ABOUT 4 CUPS

Michael's Notes: I cut the carrot and celery on the diagonal to release their flavor more quickly.

HERBES DE NAPA — This seasoning mixture is my variation on the classic *herbes de Provence*. I reach for it regularly to season lamb, roast chicken, oven-dried tomatoes, marinated cheeses, vegetable gratins, and bread stuffings.

Spring through fall, my pantry is filled with hanging bunches of drying herbs from my garden. When they're fully dry, I crumble them and combine them with some fennel seed to make this blend.

It's easy to dry your own herbs, whether you grow them yourself or buy them, but you must start with perfectly fresh specimens. Don't try to dry limp, tired herbs. Tie the stems together to form small bunches, and hang the bunches upside down in a dark, dry area with good air circulation. In a week or two, they should be dry enough to pull the leaves off the stems.

6 tablespoons dried thyme leaves

3 tablespoons fennel seed

2 ½ tablespoons dried summer savory leaves

1 ½ tablespoons dried rosemary leaves

1 ½ tablespoons crumbled bay leaves

1 ½ tablespoons dried lavender flowers (see Resources, page 210)

Combine all the ingredients. Store in an airtight container away from light and heat for up to 4 months.

MAKES 1 CUP

PICTURED ON PAGE 152

Michael's Notes: To get the most flavor from dried herbs, whether a single herb or a blend, crush them as you need them, not before. Use a mortar or a rolling pin, or simply crush them between your fingers to release the fragrance.

FENNEL SPICE — This is my favorite spice mixture. There is almost nothing it won't taste good on or in. Try it on pork ribs, chops, or tenderloin; veal chops; chicken breasts; duck; beef; liver; or eggplant. Add a pinch to lentil soup. Invite friends to a dinner featuring the spice, then send them home with a little jar as a gift.

1 cup fennel seed

3 tablespoons coriander seed

2 tablespoons white peppercorns

3 tablespoons kosher salt

Put the fennel seed, coriander seed, and peppercorns in a small, heavy skillet over moderate heat. Watching carefully, toss the seeds frequently so they toast evenly. When they are light brown and fragrant, pour them onto a plate to cool. (They must be cool before grinding, or they will gum up the blender blades.)

Pour the cooled seeds into a blender and add the salt. Blend to a powder, removing the blender from its stand and shaking it occasionally to redistribute the seeds. Store in an airtight container away from light and heat for up to 4 months, or freeze for up to 1 year.

MAKES ABOUT 1¼ CUPS

Michael's Notes: If you have a spice mill, you can cut the recipe in half. I've found that a cup is the minimum for grinding in the blender.

TOASTED SPICE RUB — I originally created a version of this spice mix for a chicken dish, but I also like to use it on lamb, shrimp, and fish. It's delicious stirred into rice, and it transforms a pot of beans. I add a pinch to soups that need a lift and to scrambled eggs and omelets.

Don't let the amount of chili powder put you off. California chili powder is almost sweet, not hot. It is not a blend of chilies and other seasonings, like the kind you would use in Texas-style chili. Instead, it is pure ground chilies. Taste your chili powder, and if it's hot, use less than the recipe indicates.

¼ cup fennel seed
1 tablespoon coriander seed
1 tablespoon black peppercorns
1½ teaspoons red pepper flakes
¼ cup pure California chili powder (see Resources, page 210)
2 tablespoons kosher salt
2 tablespoons ground cinnamon

Put the fennel seed, coriander seed, and peppercorns in a small, heavy skillet over moderate heat. Watching carefully, toss the seeds frequently so they toast evenly. When the fennel seed turns light brown, work quickly. Turn on the exhaust fan, add the red pepper flakes, and toss, toss, toss, always under the fan. Immediately turn the spice mixture out onto a plate to cool.

Pour the cooled spices into a blender and add the chili powder, salt, and cinnamon. Blend until the spices are finely and evenly ground. If you have a small spice mill or a coffee grinder dedicated to grinding spices, grind only the fennel, coriander, peppercorns, and red pepper flakes. Pour into a bowl and toss with the remaining ingredients. Keep the spice mix in an airtight container away from light and heat for up to 4 months, or freeze for up to 1 year.

MAKES ABOUT 1 CUP

Michael's Notes: Toasting releases the aromatic oils in spices, resulting in a more complex flavor.

ARBORIO RICE COATING — This is by far the best coating I know for nearly anything fried. It gives an especially crisp crust to fried fish fillets, squid, shrimp, eggplant, and veal cutlets. You may as well make a lot because it keeps well in the freezer, and it's hard to grind less than 1 cup of rice in a blender. If you have a spice mill, you can halve the recipe.

1 cup Arborio rice
3 cups unbleached all-purpose flour
1 cup semolina
2 tablespoons table salt
1 teaspoon freshly ground black pepper

Grind the rice in a blender until very fine. Put it in a bowl and add the all-purpose flour, semolina, salt, and pepper. Toss until well blended. Store in a sealed container in the freezer for maximum freshness. It will keep for months.

MAKES ABOUT 5 CUPS

Michael's Notes: This is one of the few places I use table salt. Sea salt and kosher salt are too heavy to stay evenly distributed in the coating.

PECK SEASONING—When you visit Milan, you must go to Peck, one of the most exquisite food emporia in all of Italy. Peck is where Italian gastronomes go for the fattest porcini, the freshest meats, and the most intriguing cheeses. This mixture is an interpretation of the most popular seasoning in the Peck kitchen, where my colleague David Shalleck once worked. The cooks at Peck make it in big batches once a week and use it to season everything slated for roasting: veal, rabbit, chicken, and game birds. It's also delicious on monkfish and salmon.

Be sure you chop the ingredients together, as instructed, so the flavors marry. Use the seasoning sparingly, as the mix is potent.

¼ cup minced garlic

2 tablespoons roughly chopped lemon zest

½ cup coarsely chopped fresh sage

½ cup coarsely chopped fresh rosemary

½ cup very finely minced pancetta (about 3 ounces)

¾ cup kosher salt

1 tablespoon freshly ground black pepper

Combine the garlic and lemon zest on a cutting board and chop finely. Add the sage and rosemary and mince everything together until very fine. Enjoy the aroma! Add the pancetta and mix it in well with your fingers. Add the salt and pepper and gently incorporate all the ingredients by hand until the mixture resembles a moist seasoning salt. Transfer to an airtight container and refrigerate for up to 1 week or freeze for up to 3 months.

MAKES ABOUT 2½ CUPS

PICTURED ON PAGE 26

Michael's Notes: Freeze the pancetta for 30 minutes to make it easier to mince.

PROSCIUTTO BITS—I stumbled on the idea of these tasty bits when we first started curing a lot of prosciutto at Tra Vigne, the St. Helena restaurant where I was formerly chef. We would serve the main part of the leg in large, paper-thin slices, but then we would end up with all the shanks—hundreds of pounds of meat each year that we couldn't serve. We soon solved that problem by grinding up the shank meat and using it in pasta sauces and other dishes.

One day, I was sautéing the ground prosciutto and it got too crisp. What a fortunate accident. The crisped pieces were like the ultimate bacon bits. We started sprinkling them in Caesar salads and spinach salads and on buttered asparagus. They're great in baked potatoes, in scrambled eggs, in a pasta sauce—anywhere you want crunch and a little meaty flavor.

Ask the butcher at your local deli to save the prosciutto shanks for you and to grind them on medium grind if you want to save yourself some chopping. The store probably has no use for the shanks, and you ought to be able to buy them for half the price of sliced prosciutto. I guarantee you'll have a never-ending supply of shanks if you bring some of the prosciutto bits back to the butcher.

2 tablespoons olive oil

1 pound prosciutto, preferably from the shank, very finely minced or ground with the medium blade of a meat grinder

---

Heat the olive oil in a large skillet over moderately high heat. Add the prosciutto and cook, stirring. The prosciutto will give off steam for about 5 minutes while it releases its moisture. When the hiss of steam turns to a sizzle, turn the heat down to low and cook, stirring occasionally, until the prosciutto bits are crisp, about 30 minutes.

Using a slotted spoon, transfer the bits to several thicknesses of paper towel to drain. The bits will crisp even more as they cool. Use immediately or freeze the bits for up to 6 months and warm in a skillet as needed.

MAKES ABOUT 1½ CUPS

PICTURED ON PAGE 27

Michael's Notes: Whether you are chopping the prosciutto by hand or putting it through a meat grinder, you'll have an easier time if the prosciutto is partially frozen.

LEFT: PECK SEASONING, PAGE 25; RIGHT: PROSCIUTTO BITS, PAGE 25

LEFT: *BAGNA CAUDA BUTTER*, PAGE 30; CENTER: ROASTED GARLIC THYME BUTTER, PAGE 30; RIGHT: BASIL-CHIVE BUTTER, PAGE 29

THREE FLAVORED BUTTERS—Compound butter

is a classic I learned to make years ago in cooking school, but I've

gradually updated my repertoire with more contemporary flavors.

Having these butters in the freezer is a real time-saver; all you

need is chicken breasts or some good steaks to make a great

meal in minutes. Just unwrap and slice as much butter as you

need, then rewrap and refreeze for the next time.

BASIL-CHIVE BUTTER—Slather this emerald green butter on planked salmon (page 144), steak, or scallops. Put a spoonful in a shrimp or asparagus risotto, float a slice on corn soup (page 75), or spread on toasted *pain au levain* (sourdough bread) and top with prosciutto.

4 cups firmly packed fresh basil leaves
¼ cup Basil Oil (page 31)
⅛ teaspoon powdered ascorbic acid (vitamin C)
Sea salt, preferably gray salt
1 cup (½ pound) unsalted butter, at room temperature
3 tablespoons thinly sliced fresh chives

Blanch the basil in boiling salted water just until wilted, about 10 seconds, then drain and transfer to ice water. Drain again and squeeze dry. Chop roughly.

Puree the basil, Basil Oil, ascorbic acid, and salt in a food processor. If the mixture is too dry to puree, add just enough water to ease the process. Add the butter, in tablespoon-size pieces, and puree until smooth and well blended. Taste and add more salt if desired. Transfer to a bowl and stir in the chives by hand.

Refrigerate until firm enough to shape into a log. Put an 18-inch sheet of aluminum foil on your work surface. Spoon the butter down the center of the foil into a log about 1½ inches in diameter. Enclose in foil and twist the ends to make a sealed log, like a Tootsie Roll. Refrigerate for up to 1 week, or freeze for up to 6 months.

MAKES ABOUT 1½ CUPS

PICTURED LEFT

Michael's Notes: Adding asorbic acid helps maintain the green color of the basil.

BAGNA CAUDA BUTTER—In the Piedmont region of Italy, eating *bagna cauda* is a favorite ritual. The diners gather around an earthenware pot filled with hot olive oil, anchovies, and garlic, and they dip raw vegetables or bread into the "hot bath"—a kind of Italian fondue.

I think the same seasonings make an incredible butter for flavoring cauliflower, broccoli, or stuffed baked tomatoes. Let a nugget melt onto a grilled beef steak or fish steak, or toss a generous knob into steamed clams at the last minute (page 113). Because the dish is so simple, it's critical to use extra-virgin olive oil and the best, meatiest anchovies you can find.

¼ cup extra-virgin olive oil
¼ cup chopped garlic
2 tablespoons very finely minced anchovies
1 cup (½ pound) unsalted butter, at room temperature
Sea salt, preferably gray salt
1 tablespoon very finely minced fresh Italian (flat-leaf) parsley

---

Heat the olive oil in a small saucepan over low heat. When the oil just begins to warm, add the garlic and anchovies and cook slowly, stirring, until the garlic becomes toasty brown and the anchovies dissolve, about 10 minutes. Let cool completely.

Process the butter in a food processor until smooth and creamy. Add the cooled garlic-anchovy mixture and a pinch of salt. Process until well blended. Taste and add more salt if needed. Transfer to a bowl and stir in the parsley.

Refrigerate until firm enough to shape into a log. Put an 18-inch sheet of aluminum foil on your work surface. Spoon the butter down the center of the foil into a log about 1½ inches in diameter. Enclose in foil and twist the ends to make a sealed log, like a Tootsie Roll. Refrigerate for up to 1 week, or freeze for up to 6 months.

MAKES ABOUT 1¼ CUPS

PICTURED ON PAGE 28

Michael's Notes: Add the garlic just when the oil starts to warm up. If you put the garlic in hot oil, it caramelizes too rapidly and won't flavor the oil as deeply.

ROASTED GARLIC THYME BUTTER—You'll never run out of ideas for using this seasoned butter, which you can keep in the freezer and slice as you need. I love it on mashed potatoes and tucked into baked potatoes, or as a finishing butter for risotto, swirled in at the end. You can also toss it with fresh pasta and Parmesan on one of these evenings when you don't feel like cooking, or let a nugget of it melt on a grilled New York steak. Imagine how good a burger would be if the toasted bun were spread with this butter.

1 large or 2 small heads garlic, separated into cloves and peeled
Extra-virgin olive oil
1 cup (½ pound) unsalted butter, at room temperature
1 tablespoon finely minced fresh thyme
Sea salt, preferably gray salt

Put the garlic cloves in a saucepan with just enough olive oil to cover them. Place over low heat and simmer until the cloves are soft and golden, 30 to 40 minutes. With a slotted spoon, scoop the garlic into a bowl, then mash to a puree. Immediately strain the oil through a coffee filter and reserve.

Process the butter in a food processor until smooth and creamy. Add ¼ cup of the garlic puree (save any extra for spreading on bread), 1½ tablespoons of the reserved garlic oil, the thyme, and a pinch of salt. Process until well blended. Taste and add more salt if needed.

Refrigerate until firm enough to shape into a log. Put an 18-inch sheet of aluminum foil on your work surface. Spoon the butter down the center of the foil into a log about 1½ inches in diameter. Enclose in foil and twist the ends to make a sealed log, like a Tootsie Roll. Refrigerate for up to 1 week, or freeze for up to 6 months.

MAKES 1¼ CUPS

PICTURED ON PAGE 28

BASIL OIL AND OTHER HERB OILS — This recipe gives the basic method for making a flavored oil from any herb. Because herbs vary in intensity from season to season (they tend to be mild in the spring and stronger in the fall), it's not possible to give you a recipe that will always have the perfect level of flavor. My solution is to make a concentrated essence, and then dilute it with olive oil until I get the strength I like.

I don't use extra-virgin olive oil for these infusions because I want the herb taste to be more pronounced than the olive taste. You'll need a blender; a food processor does not grind the herbs fine enough.

Herb oils are superb for drizzling on soups, sliced tomatoes, grilled meats and fish, or steamed vegetables. Don't try to cook with them, as heat kills their aroma. They are a condiment to add to a dish at the last minute.

For soft herbs, such as basil, parsley, cilantro, or tarragon, use 4 cups firmly packed leaves to 2 cups olive oil.

For woody herbs, such as rosemary, sage, thyme, oregano, or lemon verbena, use 1 cup firmly packed leaves to 2 cups olive oil.

Puree the herbs and oil in a blender until completely smooth. Put the mixture in a saucepan and bring it to a simmer over moderate heat. Simmer for 45 seconds, then pour through a fine-mesh sieve into a bowl. Don't press on the mixture, but you can tap the sieve against your hand to get the oil to drip through faster.

Immediately strain the oil again through a flat-bottomed paper filter. If the filter clogs, you may need to change the filter partway through. It's okay to pick the filter up and squeeze it gently to force the oil out faster, but be careful not to break the filter.

Sometimes a little dark liquid comes through the filter first. Don't worry; it's only water. It will settle to the bottom because it is heavier than the oil. Let the filtered oil settle for a few hours, then pour off the clear oil, leaving the dark liquid behind. Store in an airtight jar in a cool, dark place. It will stay lively for at least 1 month.

MAKES ABOUT 1⅓ CUPS

Michael's Notes: The oil passes through the filter faster if it's filtered while still hot, so set up your filter before you start the recipe. You'll need a flat-bottomed paper filter, like those used for some drip coffee machines. Cone-shaped filters tend to get clogged.

CHILI OIL — I like to use a mixture of chilies to get layers of flavor—waves of hot, fruity, roasted, and sweet. Here, I've used the mild California chili; peppery chili flakes; and the lightly smoked, ground Spanish paprika called *pimentón de la Vera*. Dried chipotles, which are smoked jalapeños, are a nice choice, but play around to find the blend you like.

½ cup pure California chili powder (see Resources, page 210)
1 tablespoon red pepper flakes
1 tablespoon Spanish *pimentón de la Vera*
2 cups olive oil

Puree the chili powder, red pepper flakes, and *pimentón de la Vera* with the olive oil in a blender until completely smooth. Put the mixture in a saucepan and bring to a simmer over moderate heat. Simmer for 45 seconds, then set aside to infuse for 10 minutes. Pour through a fine-mesh sieve into a bowl. Don't press on the mixture, but you can tap the sieve against your hand to get the oil to drip through faster.

Now strain the oil again through a flat-bottomed paper filter. If the filter clogs, you may need to change the filter partway through. It's okay to pick the filter up and squeeze it gently to force the oil out faster, but take care not to break the filter. Store in an airtight jar in a cool, dark place. It will stay lively for at least 1 month.

MAKES ABOUT 1½ CUPS

Michael's Notes: Look for California chili powder where Mexican ingredients are sold.

MY MOTHER'S TOMATO SAUCE — This is the sauce I use in my mother's *tiella* (page 178). I never asked how she made her tomato sauce, and it's too late now, but this is as close as I can get to my memory of it. It is an all-around sauce, useful to have in the freezer for quick pasta suppers or for saucing gnocchi, chicken, eggplant, or fish.

1 can (28 ounces) whole tomatoes
3 tablespoons extra-virgin olive oil
½ cup finely chopped onion
1 tablespoon minced garlic
1 bay leaf
Sea salt, preferably gray salt, and freshly ground black pepper
1 tablespoon finely chopped fresh oregano

Open the can of tomatoes and pour the juice into a bowl. Use the lid to press against the tomatoes to extract as much juice as possible. Put the tomatoes in a separate bowl, then use your hand to squeeze the tomatoes to a pulp. Reserve the juice and pulp separately. Fill the empty can half full with water and set aside.

Heat the olive oil in a heavy saucepan over moderately high heat. Add the onion and cook, stirring occasionally, until soft, about 2 minutes. Add the garlic and cook until golden. Add the tomato juice and bring to a boil. Simmer rapidly until the juice thickens, then add the crushed tomato pulp, the half can of water, the bay leaf, and salt and pepper to taste. Adjust the heat to maintain a simmer and cook, stirring occasionally to prevent scorching, until the mixture thickens and reduces to about 3½ cups, 30 to 45 minutes, adding the oregano halfway through. Discard the bay leaf.

MAKES ABOUT 3½ CUPS

MARINARA SAUCE—When the tomatoes from your garden or from the market are spectacular, make a double or triple batch of this sauce and freeze it. Then you can have dinner ready in the time it takes to cook a pot of pasta.

2 tablespoons extra-virgin olive oil
½ cup minced onion
1 tablespoon chopped fresh Italian (flat-leaf) parsley
1 large clove garlic, minced
4 cups fresh tomato puree (see Tomatoes, page 19)
1 large fresh basil stem with leaves removed
1 teaspoon sea salt, preferably gray salt
Baking soda or sugar, if needed

Heat the olive oil in a large nonreactive pot over moderate heat. Add the onion and sauté until translucent, about 8 minutes. Add the parsley and garlic and cook briefly to release their fragrance. Add the tomato puree, basil, and salt. Simmer briskly until reduced to a saucelike consistency, stirring occasionally so nothing sticks to the bottom of the pot. The timing will depend on the ripeness and meatiness of your tomatoes and the size of your pot. If the sauce thickens too much before the flavors have developed, add a little water and continue cooking.

Taste and adjust the seasoning. If the sauce tastes too acidic, add a pinch of baking soda and cook for 5 minutes more. If it needs a touch of sweetness, add the sugar and cook for 5 minutes more. Remove the basil stem before serving.

MAKES 2 TO 2½ CUPS, ENOUGH FOR 1½ POUNDS PASTA

SALSA GENOVESE—You probably know that Genoa is famous for pesto, but you might not know this other specialty, a pureed olive, nut, and herb sauce that's fantastic on fish. The men of Genoa have been fishermen and sailors for centuries, and Genoese housewives have had to devise many ways to make the catch appealing. You can spoon the sauce over any white fish—baked (see page 138), grilled, or poached—or stir some into mayonnaise as a dip for artichokes.

½ pound green olives, pitted
2 tablespoons pine nuts, toasted
2 tablespoons chopped fresh Italian (flat-leaf) parsley
2 tablespoons chopped fresh basil
1 teaspoon chopped fresh thyme (optional)
½ teaspoon grated lemon zest
½ teaspoon minced capers, rinsed before mincing
1 small clove garlic, minced
6 tablespoons extra-virgin olive oil, plus more for storing

Pulse the olives in a food processor until well chopped. Add all the remaining ingredients except for the olive oil and pulse until nearly pureed. With the machine running, add 6 tablespoons olive oil through the feed tube, pureeing until the mixture is almost smooth. Taste and adjust the seasoning.

Refrigerate in an airtight container with a thin film of olive oil on top to protect it from oxidizing. The flavors will stay lively for 2 to 3 days.

MAKES 1 GENEROUS CUP

Michael's Notes: Choose an olive that is not too heavily brined, such as Picholines or Lucques from France.

SALSA ROSA — The aroma of roasting peppers is a vivid childhood summertime memory for me. I remember big paper bags of roasted peppers cooling in our kitchen, ready to be peeled and pureed with tomatoes and chilies for this condiment. For several weeks in summer, a bowl of the sauce would be placed on the table almost every night so we could slather it on bread. We canned it for winter use, too.

I always make this sauce in quantity because it freezes well and has a million uses. You can spoon it over grilled fish or toss it with pasta. Sometimes I mix it with hummus or sour cream to make a dip, or fold it into mayonnaise for sandwiches. You can serve it with skewers of crusty grilled chicken, make a pool of it under seared scallops, or stir a little into risotto. I also whip it into unsalted butter (about ¼ cup sauce to ½ pound butter) and add some minced Calabrian chilies (see Resources, page 210) to make a superb chili butter for corn on the cob.

12 large red bell peppers

Olive oil for coating the peppers, plus 2 tablespoons, or as needed

4 serrano chilies

2 cloves garlic, thinly sliced

1 tablespoon chopped fresh oregano

1 cup fresh tomato puree (see Tomatoes, page 19)

1½ teaspoons sea salt, preferably gray salt

1 tablespoon red wine vinegar

Freshly ground black pepper

Preheat the oven to 450°F. Line a baking sheet with aluminum foil. Coat the bell peppers lightly with olive oil and place on the baking sheet. Bake, turning every 10 to 15 minutes, until the peppers are blistered all over, about 30 minutes total. Transfer the peppers to a bowl and cover with plastic wrap so they steam as they cool. Peel the peppers and remove the stems, seeds, and ribs; avoid the temptation to rinse the peppers, which would wash away flavor. You should have about 4 cups.

Heat the 2 tablespoons olive oil in a small skillet over high heat. Add the whole chilies, lower the heat to moderate, and cook, turning occasionally, until the chilies are softened, lightly browned, and blistered on all sides. Remove the skillet from the heat and let the chilies cool in the oil for several minutes. When cool enough to handle, peel the chilies and remove the stems and seeds (or leave some or all of the seeds if you prefer a spicy sauce). Chop the chilies finely, then use the side of your knife to mash them to a paste.

Add more oil to the skillet if needed to make 2 tablespoons. Reheat the oil over moderate heat and add the garlic. Cook until lightly browned, about 30 seconds, then add the oregano and sauté briefly to release its fragrance. Add the tomato puree and salt, bring to a simmer, and simmer for about 5 minutes to thicken slightly.

Combine the bell peppers, serrano chilies, and tomato sauce in a blender and puree until smooth. Add the vinegar and the black pepper to taste and puree again. Taste and adjust the seasoning. Refrigerate for up to 5 days, or freeze for up to 4 months.

MAKES ABOUT 7 CUPS

SALSA ROSA VINAIGRETTE: Puree 1 cup *Salsa Rosa*, ¼ cup extra-virgin olive oil, and 2 tablespoons red wine vinegar or balsamic vinegar in a blender until smooth. Toss with hot or cool pasta or spoon over fish.

Michael's Notes: You can roast the peppers under the broiler or over a gas flame, if you prefer, but I like to do them in a hot oven. It takes a little longer, but you don't have to monitor them as closely.

let it burn

*Don't worry if the peppers scorch in spots.
That charring enhances the flavor.*

damn hot seeds

For a milder sauce, seed the chilies.

DAMN HOT PEPPERS—My relatives on my father Fortunato's side have been making Damn Hot Peppers forever. My aunt is famous for them. Family get-togethers tend to be "sweat-offs," as one person tries to consume more Damn Hot Peppers than another.

I like to eat them with toast and cheese, which makes me think they would also be great inside a grilled cheese sandwich or a cheese omelet. Anytime you would use salsa, you can use Damn Hot Peppers—in a taco or quesadilla, or on a grilled sausage in a bun.

They last at least a week in the refrigerator, but my family cans them for even longer storage. Be forewarned: They are called Damn Hot Peppers for good reason.

¼ cup extra-virgin olive oil

3½ pounds green bell peppers, cored, seeded, and cut into 1-inch squares

½ pound jalapeño chilies, sliced crosswise into ¼-inch-thick rounds

1 tablespoon sea salt, preferably gray salt

3½ cups fresh tomato puree (see Tomatoes, page 19), or 1 can (28 ounces) whole tomatoes, pureed

---

Heat the olive oil in a large pot over moderately high heat until almost smoking. Add the bell peppers, chilies, and salt and stir to coat with the oil. Adjust the heat so the bell peppers cook without caramelizing and cook, stirring often, until they have softened, 20 to 30 minutes.

Add the tomato puree and simmer until the peppers are completely tender and the sauce has thickened, about 30 minutes, adding a little water if the sauce gets too thick before the peppers are tender. Let cool, then refrigerate.

MAKES ABOUT 7 CUPS

BOTTOM PHOTO LEFT

OVEN-DRIED TOMATOES—I have a habit of planting more tomatoes than my household can use, and when they all come ripe at once, I have to get busy. I can tomato sauce and whole peeled tomatoes, of course, but I also love to oven-dry some of them. I use a method developed by NapaStyle culinary director David Shalleck, which produces a half-dried tomato that's much moister than most commercial varieties. David seasons them with Herbes de Napa and packs them in olive oil, and they keep in the refrigerator for at least a month. I serve them alongside steaks, tuck a few inside a chicken before roasting, or cut them into slivers and add them to a sandwich.

24 plum (Roma) tomatoes, halved lengthwise

Sea salt, preferably gray salt, and freshly ground black pepper

6 tablespoons extra-virgin olive oil, plus more for storing

2 tablespoons Herbes de Napa (page 23), crushed (see Michael's Note, page 23)

1 clove garlic, minced

Preheat the oven to 250°F. Arrange the tomato halves cut-side up and close together on a baking sheet. Season with salt and pepper. In a small bowl, combine the 6 tablespoons olive oil, the herbs, and the garlic. Spoon a little over each tomato half, stirring the mixture as you go.

Bake until the tomatoes are soft and shriveled but still retain some moisture, 5 to 8 hours. Timing will depend on how large, meaty, and juicy the tomatoes are. Let cool completely, then arrange the tomatoes in a plastic container, making no more than two layers. Add olive oil to cover completely, then cover tightly and refrigerate.

MAKES 48 TOMATO HALVES

TOP PHOTO LEFT

FINE DRIED BREAD CRUMBS—I think it's ludicrous to buy bread crumbs, although I know many people do purchase them. Why spend money on an inferior product when you can make a better one almost for free? All you need is stale bread, which I always seem to have around my house. In fact, to get the finest, most delicate bread crumbs, you need very stale bread. I cut it into cubes and let it dry at room temperature for a few days or longer. If the bread isn't dry enough, the processor won't produce the lovely, silky crumbs you need for Veal Milanese with *Salsa Rosa* (page 155) and Baked Clams with Prosciutto Bits and Bread Crumbs (page 57). Just wait a day or two longer and try again.

The processor works best when it has a critical mass to work with, so make a lot of crumbs and freeze what you don't use immediately. Homemade bread crumbs freeze beautifully and are much tastier than the ones you can buy.

4 loaves (1 pound each) country-style bread

Cut the bread into 1- to 1½-inch cubes. You do not need to remove the crust. Arrange the bread cubes on trays and let stand at room temperature until very dry. This may take a day or two in hot, dry weather or up to several days if the humidity is high. In damp weather, you may need to finish the drying in a 200°F oven for about 1 hour. Let cool completely before grinding.

Working in batches, place the bread cubes in a food processor and whir until reduced to very fine crumbs. Transfer the crumbs to a large bowl. When all the bread is ground, pass the crumbs through a medium-mesh sieve, using your hand to push them through. Reprocess and resieve the crumbs that do not pass through. Discard any crumbs that don't make it through the sieve the second time. Freeze in 1- or 2-cup freezer bags for convenience.

MAKES ABOUT 9 CUPS

PANZANELLA CROUTONS—This is the basic crouton recipe I use for any *panzanella* (Tuscan bread salad), but the croutons are equally delicious sprinkled over green salads or Caesar salad. You can make them with plain unsalted butter, but I like to use a well-seasoned compound butter to give the croutons even more character.

¼ cup unsalted butter, *Bagna Cauda* Butter (page 30), or Roasted Garlic Thyme Butter (page 30)
6 cups crust-free cubed day-old bread (½-inch cubes)
6 tablespoons finely grated Parmesan cheese

Preheat the oven to 350°F.

Melt the butter in a large skillet over moderate heat and cook until it foams. Add the bread cubes and toss to coat with the butter. Transfer the bread to a baking sheet. Immediately sprinkle with the cheese and toss again while warm to melt the cheese.

Bake, stirring once or twice, until the croutons are crisp and lightly colored on the outside but still soft within, about 15 minutes. Let cool. Store in an airtight container.

MAKES 4 TO 4½ CUPS

Michael's Notes: I use a serrated knife to remove the crust from day-old bread, then switch to a chef's knife to cut the cubes because it doesn't tear the bread. Also note that I recommend grating the Parmesan finely so that it will stick to the bread better.

HOMEMADE RICOTTA — My mom usually made ricotta instead of buying it. She would mix it with honey, and we ate it on bread for breakfast. Or she would stuff her ravioli with it. It takes only about half an hour to make. The ricotta curds are very fine, so the cheese must be strained through several layers of cheesecloth or muslin. I strain mine through the same piece of muslin my mom used. Your yield will depend on the butterfat content of the milk you use. You might want to search out extra-rich milk.

1 gallon whole milk
1 quart buttermilk

Select a sieve or colander with a wide surface area so the curds will cool quickly. Rinse a large piece of cheesecloth or muslin with cold water, then fold it so that it is 6 or more layers, and arrange it in the sieve or colander placed in the sink.

Pour the milk and buttermilk into a large nonreactive saucepan. Place over high heat and heat, stirring the mixture frequently with a rubber spatula and making sure to scrape the whole pan bottom to prevent scorching. Once the mixture is warm, stop stirring. As the milk heats, curds will begin to rise and clump on the surface. As the curds begin to form, gently scrape the bottom of the pan with the spatula to release any stuck curds.

When the mixture reaches 175° to 180°F, the curds and whey will separate. The whey looks like cloudy water underneath a mass of thick white curds on the surface. Immediately remove the pan from the heat. Working from the side of the pan, gently ladle the whey into the prepared sieve. Go slowly so as not to break up the curds. Finally, ladle the curds into the sieve. Lift the sides of the cloth to help the liquid drain. Don't press on the curds. When the draining slows, gather the edges of the cloth, tie into a bag, and hang from the faucet. Drain until the dripping stops, about 15 minutes.

Untie the bag and pack the ricotta into airtight containers. Refrigerate and use within 1 week.

MAKES ABOUT 4 CUPS

Michael's Notes: I often make ricotta ravioli for the freezer. Typically, I'll boil the ravioli straight from the freezer, then simmer them briefly in chicken stock with some chard from the garden.

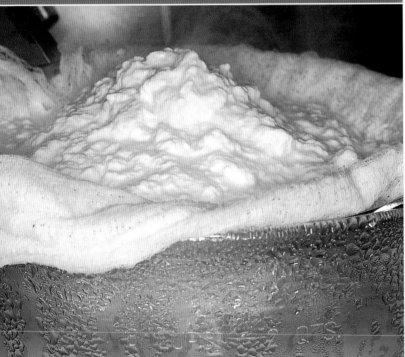

curds and whey

You can reuse the cheesecloth if you wash it well after use.

appetizers

When friends come to my house for dinner, I like to put out something a little salty to go with that first glass of wine—an antipasto that's made quickly, or already made before they arrive, to wake up their appetite. Spice-Toasted Almonds (page 42) and *Spuma di Tonno* (page 45), a creamy tuna mousse, always disappear fast. Along with the other appetizers in the following pages, they set a festive mood and make guests instantly feel welcome.

SPICE-TOASTED ALMONDS—I grew up in almond country, in California's Central Valley, and I learned from a local grower how to turn the nuts into a toasty snack. I put bowls of them out when people come for dinner, so they have something to nibble while I'm making the rest of the meal. I've learned to make the nuts in quantity because guests eat them by the handful. They taste even better when made a day ahead.

2 tablespoons unsalted butter
1 pound blanched whole almonds
2 teaspoons sea salt, preferably gray salt
1 tablespoon Toasted Spice Rub (page 24)

Preheat the oven to 350°F.

Melt the butter in a large ovenproof skillet over moderate heat and cook until it turns light brown and smells nutty. Add the almonds and salt and cook, stirring occasionally, over moderate heat until the almonds begin to color, about 5 minutes. Transfer the skillet to the oven and bake until the almonds are medium-brown, about 15 minutes.

Remove from the oven, add the spice rub, and stir to coat the nuts evenly. Return to the oven for another 5 minutes. Transfer the nuts to a sheet pan; they will crisp as they cool. Store the cooled almonds in an airtight container at room temperature.

MAKES ABOUT 3 CUPS

Michael's Notes: Chop these nuts and add them to a turkey stuffing or a rice pilaf.

BRUSCHETTA WITH HOMEMADE RICOTTA AND *SALSA GENOVESE*—My mother never served her homemade ricotta this way, but she would have liked this dish. The herbal salsa gives the mild fresh cheese the lift it needs. Even if your ricotta isn't homemade, these little *bruschette* are as close to a perfect mouthful as you can get. I serve them with Sauvignon Blanc as a *stuzzichino* (a little appetizer), but you could make a lunch out of them by adding a platter of sliced tomatoes.

2 tablespoons extra-virgin olive oil, plus more for drizzling
4 slices country-style bread, each ¾ inch thick
Sea salt, preferably gray salt, and freshly ground black pepper
¼ cup *Salsa Genovese* (page 33), at room temperature
¼ cup Homemade Ricotta (page 39), at room temperature,
   seasoned with sea salt and freshly ground black pepper

Preheat the oven to 375°F.

Heat a large ovenproof skillet over moderately high heat. Add the 2 tablespoons olive oil. When the oil is hot, add the bread to the pan and immediately turn over to coat the second side with oil. Season with salt and pepper and place the skillet in the oven. Bake for 4 minutes, then turn the slices over and bake for another 4 minutes. The toasts should have a crisp, browned exterior but should not be dried out.

Spread each slice with a tablespoon of the salsa, then top with a tablespoon of ricotta. Drizzle with a little more olive oil. Serve immediately.

SERVES 4

PICTURED RIGHT

LUCCA-STYLE ROASTED OLIVES

2 tablespoons extra-virgin olive oil

6 large cloves garlic, unpeeled, lightly crushed

5 or 6 fresh thyme sprigs

1 pint (about 2 cups) oil-cured black olives

½ pint (about 1 cup) Niçoise or Arbequina olives

4 orange zest strips

Preheat the oven to 400°F.

Cook the olive oil and garlic cloves in an ovenproof skillet over moderate heat until the cloves begin to sizzle and caramelize lightly. Add the thyme sprigs and let them sizzle in the oil for about 30 seconds. Add the olives and stir until they are hot throughout, 2 to 3 minutes. Add the orange zest.

Transfer the skillet to the oven and bake, stirring occasionally, until the olives start to soften, 5 to 8 minutes. Serve warm.

SERVES 8

warm and wonderful

Heating olives accentuates their flavor.

SALSA DI PARMIGIANO — My friend and colleague Susie Heller invented this spicy marinated cheese, which she called GLOP, when she was a caterer in Cleveland, and it was so popular that a local deli began selling it. She brings it to our company parties now, and it vanishes immediately. Susie usually serves it with warm toast, but it's also terrific in a baked potato or tossed with hot pasta. You can refrigerate it for days, but bring it to room temperature before using.

½ pound Parmesan cheese, not too dry

½ pound Asiago cheese, not too dry

2 tablespoons chopped green onion

2 teaspoons minced garlic

2 teaspoons dried oregano

1 teaspoon freshly ground black pepper

1 teaspoon red pepper flakes

1½ cups extra-virgin olive oil

Remove any rind from the cheeses and chop the cheeses into rough 1-inch chunks. Pulse the cheeses in a food processor until reduced to the size of fine pea gravel. Transfer the cheese to a bowl and stir in the green onion and garlic. Add the oregano, rubbing it between your fingers to release its fragrance. Add the black pepper, red pepper flakes, and olive oil. Stir well. Cover and let stand at room temperature for at least 4 hours before using.

MAKES 3½ CUPS, TO SERVE 16

PICTURED ON PAGE 7

Michael's Notes: The recipe specifies "not too dry" for the cheeses. A well-aged Parmesan or Asiago could break the blade on your food processor.

SPUMA DI TONNO — This smooth tuna spread is incredibly simple, yet has great depth of flavor. Everybody who tastes it asks for the recipe. I learned to make it from David Shalleck, the culinary director at NapaStyle, who learned a variation of it from Franco Colombani of Del Sole, a restaurant near Milan where David worked. I usually serve it with *grissini* (bread sticks) or *crostini* to spread it on, and I love it with Champagne. You can double the recipe easily and, believe me, it will disappear fast.

1 can (7 ounces or 200 grams) imported olive oil–packed tuna, drained

2 teaspoons fresh lemon juice

2 teaspoons soy sauce

2 teaspoons balsamic vinegar

1 tablespoon plus 1 teaspoon unsalted butter, at room temperature

Sea salt, preferably gray salt, and freshly ground black pepper

1 tablespoon heavy cream

Put the tuna in a food processor and pulse to break up the fish. With the machine running, add the lemon juice, soy sauce, and balsamic vinegar. Add the butter and blend until smooth, then stop the machine and scrape down the sides of the processor bowl. Season to taste with salt and pepper and blend again. Check the seasoning, then add the heavy cream and pulse to blend. Be careful not to overblend once the cream is added or the mixture may break.

Serve at room temperature, or cover and refrigerate for up to 4 days. If refrigerated, return the *spuma* to room temperature before serving.

MAKES ABOUT ¾ CUP

PICTURED ON FOLLOWING PAGE

Michael's Notes: Pickled caper berries make a great garnish for *spuma*.

boning up

With salt-packed anchovies, the backbone lifts out easily.

REMARINATED ANCHOVIES — These seasoned anchovies were a passion of my mother's. Often we'd be sitting around late at night and suddenly realize we were starving, so we'd open a can or two of anchovies, season them like this, and get out the bread. They are better when they have marinated for a few hours, but if you're hungry, dig in. Well covered, they'll last for a week in the refrigerator. I like to spoon them over toast topped with a slice of fresh mozzarella or to scatter them on *insalata caprese* (tomatoes, mozzarella, and basil).

12 salt-packed anchovies
¼ cup extra-virgin olive oil
1 tablespoon red wine vinegar
2 teaspoons finely minced fresh Italian (flat-leaf) parsley
½ teaspoon finely minced garlic
¼ teaspoon red pepper flakes

Rinse the anchovies under a thin stream of cold water. With your fingers, carefully slit each fish open along the belly and lift out the backbone, leaving the 2 fillets attached at the tail. Lay them skin-side down in a shallow dish. Cover with the olive oil and wine vinegar, then scatter the parsley, garlic, and red pepper flakes over them. Marinate at room temperature for 2 to 4 hours before serving, or cover and refrigerate for several hours, but bring to room temperature before serving.

SERVES 6

PICTURED ON PRECEDING PAGE

Michael's Notes: Put some spaghettini on to boil, then make a quick pasta sauce by chopping the seasoned anchovies, heating them gently in a skillet with all their oil and flavorings, and stirring until they melt. Toss the drained pasta with the hot sauce and garnish with toasted bread crumbs.

CECI ALLA SICILIANA — These marinated chickpeas, a staple of Italian-American delicatessens, don't always get the respect they deserve. Made carefully, with high-quality ingredients and attention to balance, it is a wonderful antipasto. I serve it alongside a platter of thinly sliced cured meats, like salami and prosciutto. Sometimes I'll add a can of tuna to make it into a lunch. Marinated chickpeas are also one of my favorite midnight snacks; I'm always delighted to find leftovers in the refrigerator.

2 cans (14 ounces each) chickpeas, drained and rinsed
¾ cup very thinly sliced heart of celery, including some of the chopped leaves
½ red onion, minced
3 tablespoons minced fresh Italian (flat-leaf) parsley
½ teaspoon minced Calabrian chilies (see Resources, page 210), or more to taste
1 clove garlic, very finely minced
6 tablespoons extra-virgin olive oil
1 tablespoon Champagne vinegar
Sea salt, preferably gray salt

In a large bowl, stir to combine the chickpeas, celery, onion, parsley, chilies, garlic, olive oil, and vinegar. Season to taste with salt. Serve immediately or let stand for an hour or two and reseason just before serving.

SERVES 4

PICTURED ON PAGE 51

CALABRESE ANTIPASTO — In my childhood home in California's Central Valley, this antipasto was far and away the favorite and the most frequently on the table. It was an attempt to re-create a taste my parents brought from southern Italy, using the products they could find here. You can buy a similar antipasto in many Italian delis today, but it's easy to make your own. I make it for parties because you can assemble it ahead, and the recipe makes a massive amount. My mother would can it, but it also lasts for at least a couple of weeks in the refrigerator.

Calabrese Antipasto is the comfort food I reach for when I come home from work late. With some chunks of *ciabatta* (a large, crusty, slipper-shaped loaf) and a glass of white wine, I'm content.

1 cauliflower, cut into bite-size florets

4 carrots, peeled and cut on the diagonal into ½-inch-thick slices

4 inner celery ribs, cut on the diagonal into ½-inch-thick slices

½ cup white wine vinegar

¾ pound small fresh button mushrooms

1 jar (7 ½ ounces) *peperoncini* (pickled green peppers)

1 can (7 ounces or 200 grams) imported olive oil–packed tuna, drained

1 tin (2 ounces) anchovies with capers, drained

1 can (3 ounces) pitted black olives, drained

1 jar (5 ounces) pimiento-stuffed Spanish olives, drained

1 jar (12 ounces) baby kosher dill pickles, drained and sliced ½ inch thick

1 jar (7 ½ ounces) pickled onions, drained

2 jars (6 ½ ounces each) marinated artichoke hearts, drained

ANTIPASTO SAUCE:

¼ cup extra-virgin olive oil

1 clove garlic, minced

¾ cup canned tomato sauce

½ cup ketchup

6 tablespoons fresh lemon juice

¼ cup tarragon vinegar

1½ teaspoons brown sugar

1½ teaspoons Worcestershire sauce

1½ teaspoons prepared horseradish

Sea salt, preferably gray salt

Cayenne pepper

Bring a large pot of water to a boil and salt it generously. Blanch the cauliflower for about 2 minutes; it should still be crisp. With a skimmer, transfer the florets to a tray to cool quickly. Repeat with the carrots and then with the celery, cooking them just long enough to remove their raw taste; they will be cooked more later.

Add the white wine vinegar to the water and blanch the mushrooms for 1 minute. (The vinegar will keep the mushrooms white.) Drain and spread the mushrooms on a tray to cool quickly.

Put the cauliflower, carrots, celery, and mushrooms in a large bowl. Add the *peperoncini*, tuna, anchovies, olives, pickles, onions, and artichoke hearts. Toss well.

Make the sauce: Heat the olive oil in a large pot over moderate heat. Add the garlic and sauté until golden. Add the tomato sauce, ketchup, lemon juice, tarragon vinegar, brown sugar, Worcestershire sauce, horseradish, and salt and cayenne pepper to taste. Bring the sauce to a simmer. Add the contents of the bowl. Stir well, then cover and simmer gently until the carrots are tender, 12 to 15 minutes. Cool, then refrigerate.

MAKES ABOUT 1 GALLON, TO SERVE AT LEAST 12

PICTURED ON FOLLOWING PAGE

Michael's Notes: My kids have always enjoyed making this dish with me because there are so many little jars to open. Make the recipe your own by substituting your favorite pickled or preserved foods, then passing the recipe on to your own children.

LEFT: CALABRESE ANTIPASTO, PAGE 49; RIGHT: *CECI ALLA SICILIANA*, PAGE 48

LEFT: MARINATED SALMON WITH FENNEL SALAD, PAGE 55; RIGHT: TOMATO STEAK WITH BAKED GOAT CHEESE AND HERB SALAD, PAGE 54

TOMATO STEAK WITH BAKED GOAT CHEESE AND HERB SALAD — You've probably had baked goat cheese before but never with a juicy beefsteak tomato underneath and an airy herb salad on top. I think this dish is a beautiful way to start a summer dinner, with a bottle of Pinot Grigio or Sauvignon Blanc. Edible flowers would be a nice addition to the herb salad, if you have them.

¼ cup Fine Dried Bread Crumbs (page 38)

Sea salt, preferably gray salt, and freshly ground black pepper

½ teaspoon water

1 egg

4 rounds fresh goat cheese, about 2 ounces each

4 thick, ripe beefsteak tomato slices

2 teaspoons extra-virgin olive oil, plus more for the salad

2 cups lightly packed mixed tender fresh herb leaves such as basil, chervil, tarragon, Italian (flat-leaf) parsley, chives (1-inch lengths), or young cress

Red wine vinegar

In a small, shallow bowl, mix the bread crumbs with salt and pepper to taste. Add the water and work it in with your fingers to moisten the crumbs lightly. In another small, shallow bowl, beat the egg just until blended. Dip one flat surface of each goat cheese round in the egg, and then in bread crumbs, patting the crumbs in place. Repeat on the other flat surface, leaving the sides of the rounds uncoated. Refrigerate the coated cheese rounds for about 15 minutes.

Center the tomato slices on 4 salad plates. Season with salt and pepper.

Heat a large nonstick skillet over moderately high heat. Add the 2 teaspoons olive oil. When the oil is almost smoking, add the cheese rounds, one coated-side down. Cook until lightly browned, about 45 seconds, then turn and cook on the second side until the cheese just feels quivery, about 45 seconds longer, depending on the thickness of the rounds. Place a cheese round on each tomato slice.

In a bowl, toss the herbs with a splash of red wine vinegar, a light drizzle of olive oil, and salt and pepper to taste. Mound the herbs on top of the cheese, dividing them evenly. Serve immediately.

SERVES 4

PICTURED ON PRECEDING PAGE

Michael's Notes: This salad looks best when the tomato slice and the goat cheese slice are about the same size. So if you can only find goat cheese in small logs, you may want to serve 2 goat cheese rounds to each diner and perch them on slices from small tomatoes. Be sure you take all the stems off the herbs carefully so your guests can enjoy just the soft leaves.

MARINATED SALMON WITH FENNEL SALAD— I discovered this dish on Italy's Amalfi Coast, an area famous for lemons and wild fennel. The salmon is a sort of ceviche, cooked in lemon juice with olive oil. It's best after three or four hours of marination, before the color change that marks the transformation from raw to cooked is complete.

1 pound center-cut salmon fillet, skinned and pin bones removed

1 large celery rib, sliced paper-thin on the diagonal

MARINADE:

¼ cup fresh lemon juice

¼ cup extra-virgin olive oil

1½ tablespoons chopped fennel fronds

Sea salt, preferably gray salt, and freshly ground black pepper

GARNISH:

1 fennel bulb, very thinly sliced

With a very sharp knife, trim the gray fat off the skin side of the salmon; it has a strong flavor. Slice the salmon as thinly as possible.

Make the marinade: Put the lemon juice in a small bowl. Gradually whisk in the olive oil, then whisk in the fennel fronds. Season with salt and pepper.

Arrange the salmon in an oiled dish large enough to hold the slices in a single layer. Scatter the celery over the fish, then spoon the marinade over all. Cover and refrigerate until the salmon is a little more than half cooked, which you can tell by the change in color from rosy orange to pale pink. It should take about 3 hours, depending on the thinness of the slices.

To serve, divide the salmon among 6 plates, reserving the marinade. Put the sliced fennel in a bowl and drizzle with enough of the marinade to coat it lightly. Toss well, then taste and adjust the seasoning. Divide the fennel among the plates. Spoon a little extra marinade over the salmon.

SERVES 6

PICTURED ON PAGE 52

Michael's Notes: If you're not sure how to do it, ask the fishmonger to remove the skin and pin bones from the salmon. Or you can remove the pin bones yourself with needle-nose pliers. Skin the salmon by sliding a thin, sharp knife between the skin and flesh. A mandoline or V-slicer is helpful for slicing the fennel paper-thin.

PAN-ROASTED TROUT *BRUSCHETTA* WITH CHILI VINAIGRETTE—This recipe is a contemporary variation of a dish I grew up on: *sardella*. Its aroma takes me back to my grandmother's kitchen. When the sardines were running, a family member would drive to Monterey and get a mountain of fish to divide among the extended family. The fish would be rinsed, filleted, and ground to a paste with chili powder, garlic, salt, and vinegar, then packed into a crock, covered with olive oil, and stored in the cool basement. We used *sardella* in many ways, including folding it into bread dough and baking it.

Here, I've incorporated many of the same seasonings, using trout because it's widely available. You can substitute fresh sardines or mackerel if you can find them.

1 tablespoon sherry vinegar

1 small clove garlic, minced

1 tablespoon finely chopped fresh Italian (flat-leaf) parsley

3 tablespoons Chili Oil (page 32)

Sea salt, preferably gray salt, and freshly ground black pepper

2 red bell peppers

Olive oil

8 slices country-style bread, about 6 inches long, 3 inches wide, and ½ inch thick

Extra-virgin olive oil for brushing the bread, plus ¼ cup

2 whole trout, ¾ pound each, filleted and skinned, or 4 skinless trout fillets

¾ cup Arborio Rice Coating (page 24) or Wondra flour

16 oil-cured black olives, halved and pitted

Preheat the oven to 450°F.

In a small bowl, whisk together the vinegar, garlic, and half of the parsley. Gradually whisk in the Chili Oil to make a vinaigrette. Season with salt and pepper.

Line a baking sheet with aluminum foil. Coat the bell peppers lightly with the olive oil and place on the baking sheet. Bake, turning every 10 to 15 minutes, until they are blistered all over, about 30 minutes. Transfer the peppers to a bowl and cover with plastic wrap so they steam as they cool. Peel the peppers and remove the seeds and ribs; cut each pepper lengthwise into 4 strips.

Reduce the oven temperature to 375°F.

Brush the bread on both sides with extra-virgin olive oil and season with salt and pepper. Place on a baking sheet and bake until crisp outside but still soft within, about 15 minutes.

Cut the 4 trout fillets into 8 pieces that roughly fit the toasts. Liberally salt the fish on both sides and let stand for 10 minutes to firm the flesh. Rinse well and pat dry. Dredge the fillets with the rice coating, shaking off the excess.

Heat the ¼ cup extra-virgin olive oil in a large skillet over moderately high heat. When hot, add the fish, skinned-side up, and cook until crisp, about 1 minute. Turn with an offset spatula and cook on the skinned side until done, about 1 minute. Transfer to paper towels to drain.

To serve, put 2 toasts on each of 4 plates. Top each toast with a slice of roasted pepper and a piece of trout. Spoon some of the vinaigrette over the trout. Scatter a few olives around each portion, and dust the fish with the remaining parsley. Serve immediately.

SERVES 4

BAKED CLAMS WITH PROSCIUTTO BITS **AND** BREAD CRUMBS—Everybody loves clams casino, but few restaurants make them anymore. This is my new and improved version, with salty Prosciutto Bits flavoring the bread crumb stuffing. I love the looks on people's faces when a tray of these clams goes around, because everybody remembers them.

Please don't use those awful packaged bread crumbs. It's so easy to make your own.

CLAMS:

2 tablespoons extra-virgin olive oil

2 large cloves garlic, sliced

2 pounds Manila clams (about 40) or other clams, scrubbed

1 cup dry white wine

STUFFING:

2 tablespoons extra-virgin olive oil

1 tablespoon chopped garlic

½ cup Fine Dried Bread Crumbs (page 38)

2 tablespoons Prosciutto Bits (page 25)

2 tablespoons freshly grated Parmesan cheese

2 tablespoons chopped fresh Italian (flat-leaf) parsley

Preheat the oven to 400°F.

Prepare the clams: Heat the olive oil in a large skillet over moderately high heat. Add the sliced garlic and sauté until lightly browned. Add the clams and wine and bring to a simmer. Cover and cook until the clams open, about 5 minutes, removing them to a baking sheet with a slotted spoon as they open. Discard any that fail to open. Strain the clam juices through a cheesecloth-lined sieve and reserve.

Make the stuffing: Heat the oil in a skillet over moderate heat. Add the chopped garlic and sauté until lightly browned. Add the bread crumbs, prosciutto, cheese, parsley, and ¼ cup of the reserved clam juices. Sauté until the crumbs are lightly toasted, 1 to 2 minutes.

Remove the clams from their shells and separate the shells into 2 halves. Discard the half shells with the muscle attached. Using the remaining shells, put a clam on each, or 2 clams if the clams are small. Spoon a little of the remaining clam juices over the clams. and top each with about 1 teaspoon of the seasoned bread crumbs.

Set the clams on a baking sheet and bake until hot throughout, about 5 minutes. Serve immediately.

SERVES 4 TO 6

Michael's Notes: You can steam the clams and prepare the stuffing hours ahead. Make extra bread crumbs and on another occasion, toss the seasoned bread crumbs with *Spaghettini Aglio ed Olio* (page 110) to make a terrific pasta dish.

eggs & sandwiches

Since childhood, I have thought of eggs as one of nature's most wholesome foods, and I regularly look to them for simple suppers. I grew up on frittatas (page 61), not omelets, and I now make them for my own children with whatever vegetables are in season. Along the way, I've created some of my own traditions like Green Eggs and Ham (page 63), a dish my friends and family don't easily forget.

As you'll see, I also have a passion for warm sandwiches cooked on a griddle. Whether it's a PLT (pancetta, lettuce, and tomato, page 70) or an oozy *Mozzarella in Carrozza* (page 64), I'm content to have a well-made sandwich for a weekday dinner. Like the Earl of Sandwich, who supposedly invented sandwiches so he wouldn't have to interrupt his poker game, I appreciate the ease of a sandwich supper.

ROASTED GARLIC BREAD—Roasting whole garlic cloves with rosemary, then blending the softened cloves with butter, produces a spread that makes a garlic bread to die for. Serve with soup or salad, or on its own with a robust red wine.

10 large cloves garlic, peeled but left whole

1 fresh rosemary sprig, 6 inches long

¼ cup olive oil

2 tablespoons unsalted butter, at room temperature

2 baguettes (not sourdough), ½ pound each

¼ cup freshly grated Parmesan cheese (optional)

Preheat the oven to 375°F.

Put the garlic, rosemary, and olive oil in a small ovenproof skillet and heat slowly until the oil just begins to simmer. Put the skillet in the oven and bake for 10 minutes. Turn the cloves over in the oil and bake for 10 minutes longer. Remove from the oven and let cool for 15 minutes.

Remove the garlic cloves from the oil (reserve the oil) and mash them to a paste with a knife. Take half the leaves off the rosemary sprig and finely mince them. In a bowl, combine the garlic paste, minced rosemary, and butter and stir until smooth.

Cut the baguettes in half widthwise, then lengthwise. Spread the cut sides with the seasoned butter and drizzle with a little of the oil used to bake the garlic. Arrange the halved baguettes on a baking sheet and sprinkle with the Parmesan, if using.

Bake until the baguettes begin to crisp, about 15 minutes. Cut into 2-inch-wide slices and serve immediately.

SERVES 8 TO 12

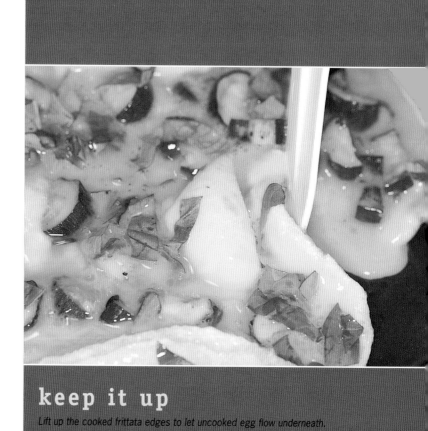

keep it up

Lift up the cooked frittata edges to let uncooked egg flow underneath.

ZUCCHINI AND BASIL FRITTATA — Make this frittata for a picnic or a summer lunch outdoors and pour a cold, crisp Pinot Grigio or Vernaccia. You can serve the frittata with toasts alongside, as the recipe describes, or you can serve the frittata wedges on the toast to make open-face sandwiches. Use this recipe as a template for other frittatas, with chopped cooked cauliflower, roasted red peppers, or sautéed mushrooms, for example.

1 pound small zucchini

1½ tablespoons extra-virgin olive oil, plus more for brushing on bread

Sea salt, preferably gray salt, and freshly ground black pepper

¼ cup coarsely chopped fresh basil

7 eggs, lightly beaten

½ cup grated Fontina or provolone cheese

8 slices country-style bread, each about ⅓ inch thick

Preheat a broiler.

Trim away the ends of the zucchini, then cut in half lengthwise. Toss with 1 tablespoon of the oil and season with salt and pepper. Arrange on a baking sheet, cut-side up. Broil until lightly browned, then turn and broil on the skin side until the zucchini are just tender. Transfer to a cutting board and slice crosswise about ¼ inch thick.

Stir the zucchini and basil into the beaten eggs. Season with salt and pepper.

Heat a 10-inch flameproof nonstick skillet over moderately high heat. Add the remaining ½ tablespoon olive oil. When the skillet is hot, add the egg mixture. Let the eggs cook without stirring until they begin to set, then lift the edges with a rubber spatula and let the uncooked egg run underneath. Continue cooking until the eggs are mostly cooked but still a little moist on top. Place the skillet under the broiler just until the surface of the frittata is no longer moist, about 30 seconds, then sprinkle the cheese on top and broil again until the cheese melts, about 30 seconds longer. Slide the frittata onto a serving plate and let cool to room temperature.

Reset the oven temperature to 375°F. Brush the bread slices on both sides with olive oil, season with salt and pepper, and place on a baking sheet. Bake until browned and crisp, about 15 minutes.

Cut the frittata into wedges to serve. Accompany each serving with 2 warm slices of toast.

SERVES 4

PICTURED LEFT

Michael's Notes: If you want to make the frittata extra light, blend the eggs for 30 seconds in a blender. Sometimes I add Prosciutto Bits (page 25) to the eggs when I add the zucchini.

GREEN EGGS AND HAM—Invite your guests for a brunch featuring this Dr. Seuss–inspired dish and they'll be talking about it for weeks afterward. I love the whimsy of the name, but even more, I love the combination of crisp toast, silky prosciutto, and soft poached egg. The basil oil ties it all together.

About 1½ quarts water

Salt

1 teaspoon white wine vinegar

2 eggs, at room temperature

2 slices country-style bread, each ½ inch thick

2 thin slices prosciutto

4 teaspoons Basil Oil (page 31)

Freshly ground black pepper

Preheat a broiler or a lightly oiled stove-top grill pan.

Meanwhile, bring the water to a boil in a medium saucepan. Salt the water, add the vinegar, then lower the heat so the water barely bubbles. One at a time, break the eggs into a custard cup or small bowl, then slide gently into the water. Allow the eggs to cook for 30 seconds, then, with a slotted spoon, gently lift and shape the whites around the egg yolks. Continue to cook until the whites are just set and the yolks are glazed but still liquid, about 2½ minutes longer.

While the eggs poach, toast the bread slices on both sides. Put a slice of toast on each of 2 plates. Immediately top with the prosciutto so that it softens from the heat of the toast. Lift the poached eggs out of the water with a slotted spoon, letting excess water drip off, then place an egg on each toast. Drizzle each toast with 2 teaspoons Basil Oil, then grind a little black pepper over each. Serve immediately.

SERVES 2

Michael's Notes: Cut the bread in such a way that each slice can accommodate a slice of prosciutto and a poached egg. A baguette won't work here; the slices would be too small.

GRILLED MOZZARELLA AND TOMATO PANINI

PANINI— My daughter Gianna and her friends love these golden brown grilled sandwiches. I make them on Saturdays while they're swimming or playing and cut the sandwiches into small triangles for easy eating. Cut small, they also make great cocktail food or a tiny, warm bite to offer guests before dinner. A whole sandwich with a green salad is a perfect quick lunch.

You'll need 2 nonstick skillets to make 4 sandwiches at once, or you can make 2 sandwiches and keep them warm in a low oven while you cook the others.

8 slices country-style bread, each ½ inch thick
½ pound whole-milk mozzarella cheese, cut into 12 slices
Sea salt, preferably gray salt
8 Oven-Dried Tomatoes (page 37)
16 large fresh basil leaves
3 tablespoons unsalted butter

First, assemble the sandwiches: On each of 4 bread slices, place 3 slices of cheese. Season with salt, then top with 2 tomato halves, 4 basil leaves, and another slice of bread.

Heat 2 large nonstick skillets over moderately high heat. When hot, add 1 tablespoon of the butter to each skillet and swirl to melt the butter and coat the skillet. Put 2 sandwiches in each skillet and place a heavy skillet on top as a weight; if the upper skillet isn't heavy, put more weight, such as canned goods, inside it. Cook until the sandwiches are well browned on the bottom, 2 to 3 minutes, then remove them. Add another ½ tablespoon butter to each skillet, and return the sandwiches, browned-side up, to the skillets. Weight as before and cook until the second side is well browned, about 3 minutes longer.

Cut the sandwiches in half on the diagonal and serve immediately.

MAKES 4 SANDWICHES

PICTURED ON PAGES 66 AND 67

Michael's Notes: If you don't have any oven-dried tomatoes, grill the sandwiches without them, then insert some fresh tomato slices.

MOZZARELLA IN CARROZZA

MOZZARELLA IN CARROZZA—A *carrozza* is a "carriage," in this case the bread that sandwiches the mozzarella and delivers it to the table. *Mozzarella in carrozza* is southern Italy's grilled cheese sandwich, with a little anchovy to cut the cheese's milky sweetness and an egg batter to make a golden coat.

You can cook 4 sandwiches at once if you have a griddle or 2 nonstick skillets. Otherwise, you'll have to cook the sandwiches in batches. Keep the first batch warm in a low oven.

4 large anchovy fillets, mashed to a paste
1½ teaspoons minced fresh oregano
¼ teaspoon minced Calabrian chilies (see Resources, page 210), or pinch of red pepper flakes
1 tablespoon extra-virgin olive oil
8 slices country-style bread, each ⅓ inch thick
⅓ pound whole-milk mozzarella cheese, thinly sliced
3 eggs
2 tablespoons milk

In a small bowl, stir to combine the anchovy paste, oregano, chilies or red pepper flakes, and olive oil. Spread one side of 4 bread slices with the anchovy mixture, dividing it evenly. Top with the mozzarella, dividing it evenly, then with the remaining bread slices.

In a shallow bowl, whisk together the eggs and milk.

Heat a large nonstick skillet or a griddle over moderate heat. When it is hot, lightly oil the griddle if it is not nonstick.

One at a time, dip the sandwiches in the egg bath, coating both sides. Set them in the skillet or on the griddle. Cook, turning once, until the bread is well browned on both sides and the cheese is molten, about 3 minutes per side. Cut in halves or quarters and serve immediately.

SERVES 4

OVEN-DRIED TOMATO *CROSTATA* — Depending on the guests, the time of the day, and the mood, I use this crostata in different ways. Sometimes I cut it into thin slivers and serve it warm with Pinot Grigio to friends as they arrive for a dinner party. For a weekend lunch or a late-night supper, I serve bigger portions with a salad of baby lettuces—maybe dandelion greens and arugula—and make it the centerpiece of the meal. The *crostata* is light and quivery and quite beautiful with the wedges of dried tomato nestled into the custard.

TART DOUGH:

2 ¼ cups unbleached all-purpose flour

1 teaspoon kosher salt

7 ounces (14 tablespoons) chilled unsalted butter, cut into tablespoon-size pieces

1 tablespoon Champagne vinegar

About 3 tablespoons ice water

FILLING:

1 ½ cups part-skim ricotta cheese

2 eggs, separated

2 tablespoons freshly grated Parmesan cheese

1 tablespoon oil from Oven-Dried Tomatoes (page 37)

Sea salt, preferably gray salt, and freshly ground black pepper

12 Oven-Dried Tomatoes (page 37), each half halved again lengthwise

Make the tart dough: In a large bowl, stir the flour and salt until blended. With both hands, work the butter into the flour until the mixture is fine-textured and no large bits of butter remain. Sprinkle the vinegar over the dry ingredients, then sprinkle the ice water, a little at a time, incorporating it with your hands and adding more water just until the ingredients come together into a dough. You may not need all the water. Knead the dough gently until it is smooth. Shape into a 1-inch-thick round, wrap tightly in plastic wrap, and refrigerate for at least 1 hour.

Preheat the oven to 375°F. On a lightly floured surface, roll out the dough into a round large enough to fit a 9-inch tart pan with a removable bottom. Carefully transfer the round to the tart pan and press into place. Trim off the overhang even with the rim by rolling the rolling pin across the rim. Put a piece of aluminum foil in the pan to cover the bottom and sides and fill with pie weights or dried beans. Bake for 20 minutes, then remove the weights and foil and

prick the shell in several places with a fork. Return to the oven and bake until lightly colored, about 5 minutes longer. Let cool before filling.

Make the filling: In a bowl, whisk together the ricotta, egg yolks, Parmesan, and tomato oil, and season with salt and pepper. Whisk the egg whites with a pinch of salt to firm peaks, then fold gently into the ricotta base. Pour the filling into the cooled tart shell, spreading it evenly. Arrange the tomato quarters, cut-side up, in 2 concentric circles, with 16 quarters on the outer circle and 8 on the inner circle. (This allows you to cut 8 portions easily without cutting through the tomatoes.)

Bake until the filling is firm to the touch and lightly colored, about 35 minutes. Cool in the pan on a rack for 20 minutes, then remove the ring and slide the tart onto a serving plate. Serve warm or at room temperature.

SERVES 8

LEFT AND RIGHT: GRILLED MOZZARELLA AND TOMATO *PANINI*, PAGE 64

DAMN HOT PEPPERS **AND POTATO HASH WITH BAKED EGGS**—At my house, eggs aren't just for breakfast. They're a protein source I turn to for quick weeknight meals, like this one. If you have eggs, potatoes, and Damn Hot Peppers on hand, you can have a nutritious dinner on the table in less than half an hour.

I like this dish best when the egg yolks are still runny, but you can cook them as firm as you like. The hash is crusty and wonderful on its own, but sometimes I'll spoon it into a flour or corn tortilla. Be sure to have plenty of beer on hand.

I use a cast-iron skillet for the hash and bring the skillet right to the table. If you can find miniature cast-iron skillets to make individual portions, you'll be a hero at brunch.

2 large russet potatoes, peeled and cut into ½-inch dice

¼ cup extra-virgin olive oil

¼ cup chopped onion

Sea salt, preferably gray salt, and freshly ground black pepper

1½ cups **Damn Hot Peppers** (page 37), at room temperature

4 eggs

1 teaspoon chopped fresh oregano

3 tablespoons freshly grated Parmesan, Asiago, or other aged cheese

---

Preheat the oven to 375°F.

Bring a pot of well-salted water to a boil. Add the potatoes and boil until about three-quarters done, about 4 minutes. Drain well.

Heat a large ovenproof skillet over high heat. When hot, add the olive oil, then add the potatoes. Lower the heat to moderate and cook, tossing occasionally, until the potatoes are crusty and browned, 10 to 12 minutes. Add the onion, season with salt and pepper, and cook until the onion browns lightly, about 2 minutes. Drain the potatoes and onion in a sieve to remove the excess oil, then return them to the skillet.

Off the heat, gently stir in the Damn Hot Peppers. If you blend them in too well, the potatoes will lose their crispness. Make 4 evenly spaced wells in the hash and break an egg into each well. Sprinkle the eggs with the oregano and scatter the cheese over the hash.

Transfer the skillet to the oven and bake until the eggs are cooked to your taste, about 6 minutes for firm whites and soft yolks. Serve immediately.

SERVES 4 AS A FIRST COURSE OR LIGHT SUPPER, OR 2 AS A MAIN COURSE

Michael's Notes: Boiling the potatoes first helps keep them from sticking to the skillet. So does preheating the pan until it's hot, hot, hot. Don't be afraid of a hot skillet. That's how chefs get such beautifully browned surfaces on foods.

PLT — You've probably figured it out already. A PLT is a BLT with pancetta in place of bacon. I've made a few other refinements, too. Instead of putting the bread in a toaster, I butter it and grill the sandwich on a griddle or in a cast-iron pan. And I weight the sandwich while I'm grilling it, which makes the bread brown better. Adding basil to the mayonnaise gives it an herbal lift, and romaine hearts contribute a fresh crunch. I love the contrast of crisp, hot, cool, and creamy in this sandwich.

¾ pound pancetta, sliced as thick as bacon

¼ cup chopped fresh basil

¼ cup mayonnaise

8 large slices country-style bread

Unsalted butter, at room temperature

12 tomato slices

Freshly ground black pepper

1 romaine lettuce heart, separated into leaves

Unroll the pancetta slices and cut into 4-inch lengths. Put the pancetta in a skillet and cook over moderate heat until it renders much of its fat and begins to crisp, about 10 minutes. Drain in a sieve.

In a small bowl, stir the basil into the mayonnaise.

Butter one side of each bread slice, then put 4 slices, buttered-side down, on a work surface. Top the bread slices with the pancetta, distributing it evenly. Top each with a second slice of bread, buttered-side up.

Heat a cast-iron skillet or grill pan until hot. Place the sandwiches in the skillet and top with a weight, such as another skillet. Cook until nicely browned, 2 to 3 minutes, then turn the sandwiches and replace the weight. Cook until the second side is well browned, about 2 minutes.

Transfer the sandwiches to a work surface and remove the top slice of bread from each sandwich. Spread the underside of those slices with basil mayonnaise. Top the pancetta with the tomato slices, pepper to taste, and romaine leaves. Replace the top slice of bread, cut the sandwiches in half, and serve immediately.

MAKES 4 SANDWICHES

Michael's Notes: You can assemble the sandwiches an hour or two before grilling them. Keep them stacked between pieces of waxed paper.

OPEN-FACE STEAK SANDWICH — Growing up in a family of modest means, I don't remember New York steak or other fancy cuts ever being on our table. I appreciate good beef now, especially when it's simply grilled, as here. But if you're not up to a splurge, you can substitute a less expensive cut, such as London broil or flank steak, with great results. Even leftover steak will work. Cold sliced beef with Damn Hot Peppers is awfully good.

This steak-and-salad dinner is a perfect summer meal for two, especially if you add a bottle of Zinfandel. Best of all, there's almost no cleanup.

1 pound center-cut New York steak, in one piece, at room temperature
Sea salt, preferably gray salt, and freshly ground black pepper
Extra-virgin olive oil
2 slices country-style bread, each about ½ inch thick

½ cup Damn Hot Peppers (page 37), finely chopped
2 cups loosely packed arugula, thick stems removed
Red wine vinegar
Wedge of Parmesan cheese

Trim excess fat from the steak, leaving a ⅛-inch border of fat. Season both sides generously with salt and pepper. Rub with olive oil on both sides.

Preheat a griddle or skillet until very hot, or prepare a hot charcoal fire in a grill, or preheat a gas grill. Cook the steak on both sides to desired doneness, about 4 minutes per side for medium-rare. Let it rest on a plate for 15 minutes while you prepare the rest of the dish.

Grill the bread on both sides until golden. Spread one side of each slice with half of the Damn Hot Peppers. In a bowl, drizzle the arugula with olive oil. Add a few drops of red wine vinegar and season lightly with salt and pepper. Toss, taste, and adjust the seasoning.

With a sharp knife, slice the steak thinly. Arrange overlapping steak slices on the prepared toasts. Drizzle the beef with any accumulated juices on the plate. Mound the arugula salad on the side. With a vegetable peeler, shave the Parmesan over the salad to taste. Serve immediately.

SERVES 2

Michael's Notes: Ask the butcher to remove the silverskin, the silvery membrane that clings to the meat. And be sure the beef is at room temperature when you cook it.

soups & salads

Every season brings fresh vegetables to celebrate in soups and salads, which are often the core of my everyday cooking. In the following pages, you'll find four produce-centered soups, from a corn soup (page 75) for a balmy August evening to a home-style onion soup (page 78) for a cold winter night. You'll also find four seasonal variations on *panzanella*, the beloved tomato-bread salad of Tuscany. Fortunately, some of the salads I love best, such as the juicy Chicken Salad with Fennel Spice (page 88), can be made and enjoyed year-round.

SPRING PEA SOUP—Fresh peas are one of those short-season vegetables that I believe in eating nearly constantly when they're around. Pureed with a few aromatic vegetables and herbs, they make a soup that's like a mouthful of spring. If you have children, enlist them to help you shell the peas, and buy a few extra so they can eat some as they go. With country bread, a wedge of cheese, and a bottle of white wine, I'd call this a meal.

3 tablespoons extra-virgin olive oil

1 clove garlic, lightly crushed

1 ½ cups sliced leek, white and pale green parts only

¾ cup diced celery

2 ¼ cups Chicken Stock (page 22) mixed with 2 ¼ cups water

½ cup heavy cream

4 ½ cups shelled English peas (about 4 ½ pounds unshelled)

3 tablespoons coarsely chopped fresh Italian (flat-leaf) parsley

1 teaspoon minced fresh thyme

⅛ teaspoon powdered ascorbic acid (vitamin C)

Sea salt, preferably gray salt, and freshly ground black pepper

Crème fraîche, Basil Oil (page 31), finely sliced fresh chives,
    or Prosciutto Bits (page 25) (optional)

Heat the olive oil in a large saucepan over moderate heat. Add the garlic and let it sizzle for about 1 minute, then add the leek and celery. Cook, stirring often, until the vegetables soften, about 8 minutes. Do not let them color. Meanwhile, pour the diluted stock into another saucepan and bring to a simmer.

Add the cream to the vegetable mixture and bring to a simmer. Add the peas and 3 cups of the simmering stock-water mixture and return to a simmer. Adjust the heat to maintain a gentle simmer and cook until the peas are just tender, about 8 minutes. Add the parsley and thyme and simmer for 1 minute longer, then remove from the heat. Transfer in batches to a blender with the ascorbic acid and puree, adding more of the stock-water mixture as needed to thin the soup to a pleasing consistency. Strain the soup through a sieve placed over a clean saucepan.

Reheat the soup slowly, but do not let it boil. Season to taste with salt and pepper. Serve in warmed bowls, garnishing as desired with a drizzle of crème fraîche or Basil Oil, or a sprinkling of chives or Prosciutto Bits.

SERVES 6

PICTURED ON PAGE 76

Michael's Notes: Ascorbic acid helps keep the green color in pureed herbs and vegetables. If you have vitamin C tablets on hand, just crush one with a rolling pin. Note that you'll need a blender to puree the soup. A food processor doesn't make it smooth enough.

SUMMER CORN SOUP—If the corn juice squirts out when you pierce a kernel with your fingernail, it's time to make this soup. I love it in glass mugs on a late-summer evening; it's equally good hot or cold. Try serving it cold in a large rimmed soup plate with a salad of diced heirloom tomatoes and herbs in the middle.

4 cups corn kernels, from about 5 ears corn (reserve the cobs)

6 cups water

½ onion, coarsely chopped

1 celery rib, coarsely chopped

1 bay leaf

½ cup heavy cream

Sea salt, preferably gray salt

Basil Oil (page 31), *Salsa Rosa* (page 34), or thinly sliced fresh chives

---

Cut the corn cobs in half widthwise and place in a pot with the water, onion, celery, and bay leaf. Bring to a simmer and cook for 15 minutes. Remove the corn cobs.

Add the corn kernels, cream, and salt to taste to the pot. Bring to a simmer and cook just until the corn is tender, about 3 minutes. Remove the bay leaf.

Transfer in batches to a blender and blend thoroughly, then strain through a fine-mesh sieve placed over a clean saucepan, pushing on the solids with a rubber spatula to extract as much liquid as possible.

Reheat the soup gently to serve. Do not allow the soup to boil, or it may curdle. Divide among warmed bowls and garnish each portion with a drizzle of Basil Oil or *Salsa Rosa,* or a sprinkle of chives. Serve immediately.

SERVES 4

PICTURED ON PAGE 77

fresh test

If a kernel squirts when you pierce it, the corn's fresh.

BUTTERNUT SQUASH AND APPLE SOUP—

The fresh acidity of fall apples helps balance the sweetness of butternut squash in this creamy autumn soup. You won't have to announce that dinner's ready. The aroma of the spice rub will lure everyone to the kitchen.

2 tablespoons unsalted butter

1½ cups sliced leek, white and pale green parts only

1 tablespoon minced garlic

6 cups peeled and roughly diced butternut squash

3 cups peeled and roughly diced apples

2 teaspoons Toasted Spice Rub (page 24)

6½ cups Chicken Stock (page 22) or 2 cans (14½ ounces each) low-sodium chicken broth mixed with 3 cups water

Sea salt, preferably gray salt

1 cup chopped Spiced Candied Walnuts (page 21) (optional)

Melt the butter in a large pot over moderate heat and cook until it turns nut brown. Add the leek and sauté until slightly softened, about 5 minutes. Add the garlic and sauté briefly to release its fragrance.

Add the squash and apples, raise the heat to high, and cook, stirring, until the vegetables begin to caramelize, about 5 minutes. Stir in the spice rub and cook briefly to toast it.

Add the stock or the broth-water mixture, bring to a simmer, and cover partially. Adjust the heat to maintain a gentle simmer and cook until the squash and apples are tender, about 40 minutes. Transfer in batches to a blender or food processor and blend until smooth. Return to the pot, reheat to serving temperature, and season with salt.

Divide the soup among warmed bowls and garnish each portion with some of the walnuts, if using. Serve immediately.

SERVES 8

Michael's Notes: Cooking the leek, squash, and apples until they caramelize gives this soup its depth of flavor.

ITALIAN HOME-STYLE ONION SOUP—Known

in Italian as *pappa alle cipolle*, this soul-warming soup makes a nourishing weeknight supper. Use any combination you like: yellow onions, red onions, leeks, shallots, cipolline, even green onions. The colder it is outside, the more I caramelize the onions.

2 tablespoons extra-virgin olive oil

1 tablespoon minced garlic

8 cups thinly sliced onions

Sea salt, preferably gray salt

1 tablespoon finely chopped fresh sage

¼ cup balsamic vinegar

4 cups Chicken Stock (page 22)

½ recipe *Panzanella* Croutons (page 38)

¼ pound Fontina cheese, thinly sliced

Heat the olive oil in a large skillet over high heat. Add the garlic and cook briefly to release its fragrance. Add the onions and a little salt to help the onions release their liquid. Cook briskly, stirring often, for about 7 minutes, then reduce the heat to moderate and cook, stirring occasionally, until the onions are golden brown, about 25 minutes more.

Add the sage and vinegar and cook until the liquid evaporates. Add the stock and simmer for 10 minutes.

Preheat the broiler. Transfer the soup to a flameproof serving dish. Bring to a boil on the stove. Top with croutons, then with the Fontina. Broil until the cheese melts, then serve immediately.

SERVES 4

PICTURED RIGHT

Michael's Notes: For this dish and many others, I slice the onions in a particular way that I've come to call onion-soup style. Slice off both ends, then halve lengthwise and peel. Now slice thinly lengthwise (from stem end to root end), not crosswise. This method gives you shorter, more even slices instead of long, stringy slivers that can be unpleasant to eat, especially in a soup.

WARM POTATO-TOMATO SALAD WITH DIJON VINAIGRETTE — Although everybody, deep down, loves potato salad, I think people have largely moved away from the heavier mayonnaise versions. I make mine with a creamy Dijon vinaigrette and brighten it with tarragon and fresh tomato. Take it to a picnic or potluck and watch it disappear.

Replace the diced tomato with halved cherry tomatoes, if they're available and sweet. If you have leftover vinaigrette, save it for tomato salads or green beans.

VINAIGRETTE:

3 tablespoons Dijon mustard

2 tablespoons red wine vinegar

½ teaspoon sea salt, preferably gray salt

½ cup extra-virgin olive oil

Freshly ground black pepper

2 pounds Yukon Gold potatoes, skin on, cut into 1-inch chunks

2 cups diced tomato, skin on, including seeds and juice

½ cup finely minced red onion

2 teaspoons finely minced fresh tarragon

Make the vinaigrette: In a bowl, whisk together the mustard, vinegar, and salt. Whisk in the olive oil gradually, then season with pepper.

Put the potatoes in a large pot of cold, well-salted water to cover. Bring to a boil, adjust the heat to maintain a gentle simmer, and cook until tender when pierced, about 15 minutes. Drain well and transfer to a large bowl to cool slightly.

Add some of the vinaigrette to the potatoes and toss; you may not need it all. Add the tomato, onion, and tarragon and toss again. Taste and adjust the seasoning. The salad will probably need more salt.

SERVES 6

Michael's Notes: Be sure to use well-salted water when you boil the potatoes. It's your only chance to get salt *into* the potatoes, instead of on them.

RADICCHIO SLAW WITH WARM HONEY DRESSING—The more I learn about the cooking of the southern United States, the more I see similarities with southern Italy. Both regions love sweet-and-sour flavors, for example. Southern Americans have their sweet-tart cabbage slaws and their vinegary barbecue sauces, while southern Italians have a whole repertoire of *agrodolce* (bittersweet) dishes based on vinegar and sugar.

This *agrodolce* slaw is one I created to accompany barbecued ribs, but it would be great with just about anything off the grill, like sausages, pork chops, or chicken.

1 medium head radicchio	DRESSING:
½ head Napa cabbage	2 teaspoons fennel seed
Ice water	3 tablespoons honey
1 bunch watercress	3 tablespoons Champagne vinegar
	½ cup extra-virgin olive oil
	Sea salt, preferably gray salt, and freshly ground black pepper

Cut the radicchio into 4 wedges through the core, then remove the core. Slice the leaves into ⅛-inch-wide ribbons. Halve the cabbage through the core, remove the core, and slice like the radicchio. Put the radicchio and cabbage in a large bowl, cover with ice water, and soak for 20 minutes. Drain and repeat. Drain again, pat dry, and set aside. Trim the thick stems from the watercress and set aside.

Make the dressing: Toast the fennel seed in a small skillet over moderately low heat until fragrant and lightly colored, 3 to 5 min-utes. Let cool, then crush the seed in a mortar or grind in a spice grinder.

Combine the honey, vinegar, and ground fennel in a small saucepan. Bring to a boil, stirring until the honey dissolves. Remove from the heat and whisk in the olive oil. Season with salt and pepper.

Toss the radicchio, cabbage, and watercress in a large bowl. Add enough of the warm dressing to coat the salad; you may not need it all. Toss well, then taste and adjust the seasoning. Serve immediately.

SERVES 6 TO 8

Michael's Notes: Soaking the radicchio and cabbage in ice water crisps them both and removes any bitterness from the radicchio. It's a technique I use whenever I'm putting radicchio in a salad.

crisp and crunchy

Soaking radicchio in ice water removes bitterness and makes it crisp.

RIGHT: WHOLE-LEAF CAESAR SALAD, PAGE 83

WHOLE-LEAF CAESAR SALAD—You've probably made Caesar salad at home, and you probably have an opinion about what makes a great one. I like to use crisp, whole leaves of romaine taken just from the pale heart, and I like to make my dressing in the blender so it's thick and creamy. This recipe makes twice as much dressing as you need, but you can't split an egg yolk. The extra dressing will keep for a week in the refrigerator, giving you a head start on another Caesar.

DRESSING:

1 egg yolk

1 tablespoon Dijon mustard

3 or 4 anchovy fillets, minced

1 tablespoon chopped garlic

2 tablespoons balsamic vinegar

1½ teaspoons fresh lemon juice

Worcestershire sauce

1 cup olive oil

1 tablespoon warm water, if needed

½ cup freshly grated Parmesan cheese

SALAD:

2 heads romaine lettuce, outer leaves removed, or ¾ pound romaine lettuce hearts

¾ cup dressing (see left)

8 Parmesan Toasts (page 84)

1 tablespoon freshly grated Parmesan cheese

Make the dressing: Place the egg yolk, mustard, anchovies, garlic, vinegar, lemon juice, and a dash of Worcestershire sauce in a blender. Blend until pureed. With the motor running, add the olive oil in a slow, steady stream until it is fully incorporated. If the dressing stops moving in the blender, stop the machine, add the warm water, and then continue until all the oil is added. Add the cheese and blend on low speed to incorporate. Makes about 1½ cups.

Make the salad: Put the whole romaine leaves in a work bowl. Add enough of the dressing to coat the leaves and toss well. Arrange the leaves in a serving bowl with their tips up, and intersperse the toasts. Sprinkle the Parmesan over all.

SERVES 4

PICTURED LEFT

Michael's Notes: I'll put knives and forks on the table, but to me, this is a perfect salad to eat with your fingers.

PARMESAN TOASTS— These thin, crisp toasts are terrific floated on onion soup or tomato soup. I also use them to garnish salads and sometimes serve them before dinner with red wine. You'll need a sharp serrated knife to slice the bread very thinly.

½ pound day-old country-style bread, sliced ⅛ inch thick
Extra-virgin olive oil
½ cup freshly grated Parmesan cheese

Preheat the oven to 300°F.

Brush one side of each bread slice with olive oil. Dust the oiled side with the Parmesan. Arrange on a baking sheet and bake until golden brown and crisp, 20 to 25 minutes. Serve warm or at room temperature.

MAKES 20 TO 24 SLICES

Michael's Notes: If you use a baguette and slice it on an extreme diagonal, you can make long toasts that look dramatic poking out of a salad bowl.

WARM PEACH AND PROSCIUTTO SALAD— You've probably had prosciutto with melon, and maybe with figs. If you like those pairings, you'll love this one: prosciutto with peaches sizzled in brown butter until they're warm outside but cool and silky within.

⅓ pound very thinly sliced prosciutto
1 pound peaches, at room temperature, peeled and each cut into 8 wedges
Sea salt, preferably gray salt, and freshly ground black pepper
2 ½ tablespoons unsalted butter
1 bay leaf
2 teaspoons finely minced fresh thyme
2 tablespoons balsamic vinegar
4 cups loosely packed arugula

Cut the prosciutto slices in half crosswise and arrange them in a fan on 4 dinner plates, dividing them equally.

Put the peaches in a bowl and season with salt and pepper.

Melt the butter in a large skillet over moderate heat. When the butter turns light brown, add the bay leaf, thyme, peaches, vinegar, and salt and pepper to taste. Toss for about 45 seconds. Remove the bay leaf.

Remove from the heat, add the arugula, and toss with tongs until the arugula wilts slightly. Divide the arugula and peaches among the 4 plates and serve immediately.

SERVES 4

PICTURED RIGHT

FRISÉE SALAD WITH SPICED WALNUTS, PEARS, BLUE CHEESE, AND PORT VINAIGRETTE

My colleague Susie Heller showed me how to make a snowlike flurry of blue cheese on a salad by freezing the cheese first. You can use any blue, but I'm in love with Point Reyes Original Blue (see Resources, page 210), a new cheese from the dairy country north of San Francisco.

Baby greens, pears, walnuts, and blue cheese are a classic autumn combination, but the spiced walnuts and the Port vinaigrette set this salad apart.

DRESSING:

1 cup Port

1½ tablespoons red wine vinegar

1 shallot, finely minced

Sea salt, preferably gray salt, and freshly ground black pepper

6 tablespoons extra-virgin olive oil

SALAD:

8 cups loosely packed young frisée (curly endive), torn into bite-size pieces, or mesclun

1½ cups ribbon-cut radicchio, soaked, drained, and dried (see Radicchio Slaw with Warm Honey Dressing, page 81)

1 crisp red pear, halved, cored, and very thinly sliced crosswise

2-ounce chunk blue cheese, frozen

½ cup coarsely broken Spiced Candied Walnuts (page 21)

Make the dressing: Simmer the Port in a small saucepan until reduced to 2 tablespoons. Let cool, then whisk in the wine vinegar, shallot, and salt and pepper to taste. Gradually whisk in the olive oil.

Make the salad: In a large bowl, toss the frisée, radicchio, and pear. Divide the salad among 4 plates. Drizzle with the dressing; you probably won't use it all. Using the medium holes of a box grater, shave the blue cheese in a fine snowlike shower over the salads. Scatter the walnuts on top and serve immediately.

SERVES 4

PICTURED RIGHT

Michael's Notes: Supermarket pears are usually rock hard because they have just come out of cold storage. Buy your pear a couple of days before you plan to use it, and leave it at room temperature to soften a little. It's easier to slice if it's still fairly firm.

blue ice

I use a microplane grater to make a
snowlike flurry of blue cheese on this salad.
It helps to freeze the cheese briefly first.

CHICKEN SALAD WITH FENNEL SPICE—Rather than making chicken stock the restaurant way, with bony necks and backs, I'm fond of making a rich stock using a whole bird. Every so often, I'll make a batch and fill my freezer, leaving me with the dividend of a lot of poached chicken. I'll shred the moist meat by hand, combine it with celery heart and red onion, and dress the mixture liberally with my best olive oil, lemon juice, and—the secret ingredient—Fennel Spice. It couldn't be easier or better, but you could add some greens or radicchio to make it more substantial, or you could spoon the chicken over *bruschetta*.

BOILED CHICKEN:

1 chicken, about 3 ½ pounds

1 large celery rib, halved

1 large carrot, halved

1 large yellow onion, quartered

2 bay leaves

¼ cup thinly sliced celery heart

¼ red onion, thinly sliced onion-soup style
  (see Michael's notes, page 78)

6 to 7 tablespoons extra-virgin olive oil

2 to 3 tablespoons fresh lemon juice

1 ½ teaspoons Fennel Spice (page 23), or more to taste

Sea salt, preferably gray salt, and freshly ground black pepper

¼ cup thinly sliced fresh basil

Prepare the chicken: Put the chicken, celery rib, carrot, yellow onion, and bay leaves in a pot just large enough to hold them comfortably. Add cold water to cover. Bring to a simmer, skimming any foam. Adjust the heat to maintain a bare simmer and cook, uncovered, for 1 hour. Remove from the heat and let cool in the liquid. Lift out the cooled chicken and strain the stock, discarding the solids. Refrigerate or freeze the chicken stock for another use.

Remove the skin and bones from the chicken. Shred the meat by hand into rough bite-size pieces.

In a large bowl, combine the shredded chicken, celery heart, red onion, 6 tablespoons olive oil, 2 tablespoons lemon juice, 1 ½ teaspoons Fennel Spice, and salt and pepper to taste. Taste and add more oil, lemon juice, or Fennel Spice, if desired. Add the basil and serve.

SERVES 4 TO 6

Michael's Notes: It's important to simmer the chicken slowly to keep it tender. To slice fresh basil thinly in what professional cooks call a *chiffonade*, stack several leaves together, then roll them up like a cigar and slice thinly crosswise.

SHAVED CARROT, FENNEL, AND TANGERINE SALAD—This salad is drop-dead gorgeous. You'll want to serve it in a clear glass bowl so guests can admire its beautiful spring colors. You could serve it for lunch with some chilled shrimp or thinly sliced ham, for Easter dinner with a glazed ham, or as an accompaniment to Forever-Roasted Pork with Toasted Spice Rub (page 161). I use bunch carrots with tops attached because they tend to be sweeter and more tender than the bigger bulk carrots.

Note that you'll need a manual vegetable slicer, such as a mandoline or V-slicer, to shave the vegetables into paper-thin ribbons.

½ pound bunch carrots with tops attached

2 medium fennel bulbs

3 tablespoons extra-virgin olive oil

2 tablespoons fresh lemon juice

1 tablespoon Champagne vinegar, or as needed

¼ medium red onion, thinly sliced onion-soup style
   (see Michael's Notes, page 78)

1 cup tangerine sections

2 cups watercress sprigs, thick stems removed

Sea salt, preferably gray salt, and freshly ground black pepper

---

Remove the carrot tops and peel the carrots. Cut them into 3-inch lengths, then use a manual vegetable slicer to shave them lengthwise into ribbons. Cut off the stalks and fronds from the fennel bulbs if still attached, then halve the bulbs. Remove the outer layer, which is usually tough. Shave the fennel lengthwise like the carrots.

Put the carrots and fennel in a bowl and toss with the olive oil, lemon juice, and 1 tablespoon vinegar. Let stand for 20 minutes to soften.

Add the red onion, tangerine sections, and watercress. Season with salt and pepper, toss well, taste, and add more vinegar if needed. Serve immediately.

SERVES 6

Michael's Notes: If your tangerines are small, you can leave the sections intact. If the tangerines are large, or if you want to use oranges, you should remove each citrus section from its membrane. To do so, cut a slice off both ends of each fruit so it will stand upright. Stand each fruit on a cutting surface and, using a sharp knife, remove all the peel and white pith by slicing from top to bottom all the way around the fruit, following its contours. Cut the sections away from their membranes.

BITTER GREENS WITH POACHED EGGS AND PROSCIUTTO BITS — This is one of my favorite too-tired-to-cook suppers. Even when I'm running on empty, I can poach an egg. With some country bread and a sliced tomato, this salad satisfies me completely. The recipe makes a generous amount of mustard tarragon dressing, which you can spoon over poached leeks, roasted beets, or steamed cauliflower the next day. It's a great dressing to have in your repertoire.

When friends come for dinner, you can reduce the amount of greens and serve this dish as a first course.

DRESSING:

¼ cup Dijon mustard

2 tablespoons sherry vinegar

½ teaspoon sea salt, preferably gray salt

½ cup extra-virgin olive oil

1 tablespoon chopped fresh tarragon

4 quarts water

¼ cup white wine vinegar or Champagne vinegar

1 tablespoon sea salt, preferably gray salt

4 eggs

½ pound mixed bitter greens such as frisée, mizuna, radicchio, and arugula

½ cup Prosciutto Bits (page 25)

Freshly ground black pepper

Make the dressing: In a small bowl, whisk together the mustard, sherry vinegar, and salt. Gradually whisk in the olive oil to make an emulsion, then whisk in the tarragon.

Bring the water to a boil in a deep saucepan. Add the wine vinegar and salt. Adjust the heat so the water barely bubbles. One at a time, break the eggs into a custard cup or small bowl, then slide gently into the water. Allow the eggs to cook for 30 seconds, then, with a slotted spoon, gently lift and shape the whites around the yolks. Continue to cook until the whites are just set and the yolks are glazed but still liquid, about 2½ minutes longer. Transfer the poached eggs with a slotted spoon to a clean dish towel or paper towels to drain.

In a large bowl, toss the greens with enough of the dressing to coat them lightly. Taste and adjust the seasoning. Divide the greens evenly among 4 plates. Top each salad with a warm poached egg, 2 tablespoons Prosciutto Bits, and a grinding of black pepper. Serve at once.

SERVES 4

Michael's Notes: Eggs poach best when the water is relatively deep, so use a deep saucepan. Adding vinegar to the water helps to set the whites.

LEFT: WINTER *PANZANELLA*, PAGE 96; RIGHT: SPRING *PANZANELLA*, PAGE 97

PANZANELLA TUTTI STAGIONI—Italians make

panzanella—bread salad—only in summer when they can get juicy,

ripe tomatoes to moisten the bread. But I've always thought

panzanella was a dish that could change with the seasons, using

whatever vegetables were freshest. The idea is simple: rescue

stale bread by first making it into savory croutons, and then incor-

porate the croutons into a salad of seasonal ingredients. I've

improvised on this theme many times. Here are a few of my

favorites.

SUMMER *PANZANELLA*—The classic *panzanella* is made with moistened stale bread mixed with fresh basil and chopped tomatoes. I like it better with crunchy croutons that are just slightly softened by the tomato juices.

2 pounds ripe tomatoes, peeled, seeded, and diced
¼ cup minced red onion
2 teaspoons minced garlic
½ cup extra-virgin olive oil
2 tablespoons fresh lemon juice
2 tablespoons chopped fresh basil
1 tablespoon chopped fresh tarragon
1 teaspoon sea salt, preferably gray salt
Freshly ground black pepper
***Panzanella* Croutons (page 38)**
2 cups arugula
Wedge of Parmesan cheese

Drain the tomatoes in a sieve to remove excess liquid while you prepare the rest of the ingredients.

In a bowl, combine the tomatoes, onion, garlic, olive oil, lemon juice, basil, tarragon, salt, and pepper to taste. Add the croutons and toss well.

Divide among 4 plates. Top each serving with an equal amount of the arugula. With a vegetable peeler, shave the Parmesan over the salad. Serve immediately.

SERVES 6 AS A FIRST COURSE OR SIDE DISH, OR 4 AS A MAIN COURSE

PICTURED ON PAGE 92

Michael's Notes: I've used basil and tarragon here, but you can use any herbs you like. Parsley and marjoram come to mind as good alternatives.

AUTUMN *PANZANELLA* — This warm mushroom bread salad could be a meal in itself or a side dish for game, roast chicken, or the Thanksgiving turkey.

1 tablespoon unsalted butter

1 yellow onion, coarsely chopped

3 tablespoons red wine vinegar

8 tablespoons extra-virgin olive oil

2 tablespoons warm water

Sea salt, preferably gray salt, and freshly ground black pepper

1 pound fresh wild mushrooms, thickly sliced or quartered

1 tablespoon finely minced fresh thyme

1 tablespoon finely minced garlic

Panzanella Croutons (page 38)

¾ cup thinly sliced celery heart (on the diagonal), plus some chopped leaves

¼ red onion, very thinly sliced onion-soup style (see Michael's Notes, page 78)

2 ounces baby arugula or spinach leaves

Melt the butter in a small skillet over moderately low heat. Add the yellow onion and sauté until soft, about 15 minutes. Add the vinegar and stir with a wooden spoon to release any browned bits stuck on the bottom of the skillet. Transfer to a blender or food processor and puree until smooth. With the machine running, slowly add 5 tablespoons of the olive oil, then the water. Transfer to a bowl and season with salt and pepper.

Heat a large skillet over high heat. When hot, add the remaining 3 tablespoons oil. When the oil begins to smoke, sprinkle in the mushrooms. Don't stir! Let them sizzle until they have caramelized on the bottom, about 2 minutes. If you toss them too soon, they will release their liquid and begin to steam. When the bottoms are caramelized, toss the mushrooms, reduce the heat to moderate, and continue to cook until well browned. Stir in the thyme and garlic and cook for about 1 minute to release their fragrance. Season with salt and pepper.

In a large bowl, combine the croutons, the mushrooms, and the onion dressing. Toss well to coat. Add the celery, red onion, and arugula or spinach and toss again gently. Taste and adjust the seasoning. Serve immediately.

SERVES 6 AS A FIRST COURSE OR SIDE DISH, OR 4 AS A MAIN COURSE

PICTURED ON PAGE 92

WINTER *PANZANELLA* — Roasted butternut squash and slivers of Brussels sprouts put this *panzanella* in a winter mood. I would serve it with roast pork, quail, or squab, or with a slice of Taleggio for a simple supper.

4 cups peeled and diced butternut squash (½-inch dice)

½ cup plus 2½ tablespoons extra-virgin olive oil

1 tablespoon chopped fresh sage

Sea salt, preferably gray salt, and freshly ground black pepper

½ pound Brussels sprouts, ends trimmed, then thinly sliced lengthwise

½ red onion, sliced onion-soup style (see Michael's Notes, page 78)

3 tablespoons sherry vinegar

Panzanella Croutons (page 38)

½ cup fresh Italian (flat-leaf) parsley leaves

Preheat the oven to 400°F. Toss the squash with 1½ tablespoons of the olive oil. Add the sage and salt and pepper to taste and toss again. Arrange in a single layer on a baking sheet and bake until the squash is tender and lightly caramelized, about 30 minutes. Let cool.

Bring a large pot of salted water to a boil. Add the Brussels sprouts and cook until they are tender but retain a touch of crispness, about 3 minutes. Drain.

To make a vinaigrette, soak the onion in the sherry vinegar for about 15 minutes to mellow it, then whisk in the remaining ½ cup plus 1 tablespoon oil. Season with salt and pepper.

In large bowl, combine the croutons, the squash, and the Brussels sprouts. Add the vinaigrette and toss. Add the parsley leaves and toss again. Taste and adjust the seasoning. Serve immediately.

SERVES 6 AS A FIRST COURSE OR SIDE DISH, OR 4 AS A MAIN COURSE

PICTURED ON PAGE 93

Michael's Notes: Soaking the onion briefly in sherry vinegar—sometimes called blooming the onion—mellows the raw onion taste.

SPRING *PANZANELLA* — Tossing the croutons with asparagus, radicchio, spinach, and peas makes a wildly colorful spring creation, with snowy shavings of ricotta salata on top.

Serve this salad with grilled salmon or lamb chops, or have it for lunch with some sliced prosciutto. If you have any leftover dressing, save it for a salad the next day.

1 pound medium asparagus

$\frac{1}{8}$ teaspoon powdered ascorbic acid (vitamin C)

$\frac{1}{4}$ cup chopped fresh basil

4 tablespoons extra-virgin olive oil

Sea salt, preferably gray salt, and freshly ground black pepper

Panzanella Croutons (page 38)

1 cup fresh or frozen English peas, boiled until tender and drained

$\frac{1}{2}$ cup thinly sliced green onion

1 $\frac{1}{2}$ tablespoons plus $\frac{1}{2}$ teaspoon fresh lemon juice

$\frac{1}{4}$ head radicchio, ribbon-cut, soaked, drained, and dried (see Radicchio
    Slaw with Warm Honey Dressing, page 81)

1 cup whole baby spinach leaves or arugula

Wedge of ricotta salata cheese

Holding an asparagus spear in both hands, bend the spear until it breaks naturally at the point where the spear becomes tough. Discard the tough end. Repeat with the remaining asparagus. Cut off the tender tips and reserve.

Bring a large pot of salted water to a boil over high heat. Add the asparagus tips and cook briefly, just until they lose their raw taste. Lift them out with a sieve or skimmer and let cool. Add the remaining portion of the asparagus spears and cook until tender enough to puree, then drain well.

Put the asparagus spears in a blender or food processor with the ascorbic acid, basil, 3 tablespoons of the olive oil, and salt and pepper to taste. Puree until smooth.

In a large bowl, combine the croutons, asparagus tips, peas, and green onion. Add some of the asparagus puree and toss to coat well. Add more puree as needed to coat lightly and evenly. Add 1 $\frac{1}{2}$ tablespoons of the lemon juice and toss again. Taste and adjust the seasoning, then make an even layer of the mixture on a platter.

In another bowl, combine the radicchio and the spinach or arugula. Dress with the remaining 1 tablespoon olive oil, the remaining $\frac{1}{2}$ teaspoon lemon juice, and salt and pepper to taste. Toss well, then mound on top of the dressed croutons. With a cheese plane or vegetable peeler, shave some ricotta salata over the top. Serve immediately.

SERVES 6 AS A FIRST COURSE OR SIDE DISH, OR 4 AS A MAIN COURSE

PICTURED ON PAGE 93

p a s t a

Pasta is my passion, my mainstay, my fallback position. When I'm tired or stressed or happy or just hungry, I cook pasta. Although I'm inclined to improvisation, I've also codified a number of the sauces that my friends and family have most enjoyed over the years. Included in the following pages are four fast variations on Bolognese sauce, the slow-cooked meat sauce of Emilia-Romagna; as well as three pestos that, side by side, repeat the colors of the Italian flag.

FOUR BOLOGNESE SAUCES — When I have time, I love to make the classic Bolognese sauce from Emilia-Romagna, a slowly simmered and well-seasoned blend of chopped beef and finely diced vegetables. But when I don't have time, I make a quick version, borrowing the idea of mincing all the ingredients but then improvising the rest. The four Bolognese variations that follow may not simmer for hours, but they are packed with flavor and perfect for weeknight pasta dinners.

soak up the flavor
It's worth seeking out dried porcini mushrooms. They have a rich and unique flavor.

PAPPARDELLE WITH VEAL AND PORK BOLOGNESE, PAGE 102

PAPPARDELLE WITH VEAL AND PORK BOLOGNESE — The classic, ultra-rich Bolognese sauce takes hours of gentle simmering, which means that, for me, it's a weekend dish only. Here's a lighter weekday variation, made in about the time it takes to cook the pasta. The Marinara Sauce (or pureed tomato) is merely a background note; it shouldn't take over the sauce.

I prefer this Bolognese sauce on fresh pasta, preferably on a wide noodle like *pappardelle* or the somewhat slimmer fettuccine, but dried pasta is also okay. I also love the sauce stirred into risotto or spooned over a bowl of creamy polenta.

¼ ounce dried porcini

½ cup warm water

6 tablespoons extra-virgin olive oil

½ cup chopped onion

1 tablespoon minced garlic

1 teaspoon minced fresh rosemary

½ pound ground veal

¼ pound ground pork

Sea salt, preferably gray salt, and freshly ground black pepper

⅓ cup dry white wine

¾ cup veal stock or Chicken Stock (page 22)

1 tablespoon finely chopped fresh Italian (flat-leaf) parsley

½ cup Marinara Sauce (page 33) or tomato puree
   (see Tomatoes, page 19)

¾ pound fresh *pappardelle* or fettuccine

2 tablespoons freshly grated Parmesan cheese, plus more for garnishing

---

In a small bowl, rehydrate the porcini in the ½ cup warm water for 30 minutes. Lift the porcini out with a slotted spoon and chop finely. Strain the liquid through a double thickness of damp paper towels to catch any grit. Reserve the porcini and liquid separately.

Bring a large pot of salted water to a boil over high heat.

Meanwhile, heat the olive oil in a large skillet over moderate heat. Add the onion and sauté gently until softened, about 5 minutes. Do not let it color. Add the garlic and rosemary and sauté briefly to release their fragrance.

Add the veal and pork and cook, breaking the meat apart with a wooden spoon, until it loses its pinkness. Season with salt and pepper. Add the porcini and cook until any moisture evaporates and the meat begins to sizzle. Raise the heat to moderately high, add the wine and 2 tablespoons reserved porcini liquid, and cook for a minute or two to evaporate the liquid. Add the stock and pars-

ley and simmer briskly for 2 minutes. Add the Marinara Sauce or tomato puree, reduce the heat to a gentle simmer, and cook for 3 to 4 minutes to blend the flavors. Keep the sauce warm while you cook the pasta.

Add the pasta to the boiling water and cook until it is just shy of al dente. Set aside 1 cup of the pasta water, then drain the pasta. Return the pasta to the warm pot over moderately low heat. Add the sauce, stir well, and cook the pasta briefly so it absorbs some of the sauce. Add the 2 tablespoons Parmesan and toss again, adding some of the reserved pasta water if the sauce appears dry.

Transfer the pasta to a warmed serving bowl, garnish with a little additional Parmesan, and serve at once.

SERVES 4

PICTURED ON PRECEEDING PAGE

Michael's Notes: Don't leave any flavor behind in the skillet. After you put the pasta on the plates, rinse the pan with a little of the pasta cooking water, *mescola bene* (mix well), and pour that bit of concentrated sauce over the top of the pasta.

TRENNE WITH SHRIMP BOLOGNESE — My shrimp Bolognese might raise a few eyebrows in Emilia-Romagna, where a Bolognese sauce is always made with meat and simmered for hours. Obviously I've taken a few liberties, but I've done so in the interest of producing a fast and delicious pasta sauce in the same style. My version uses the Bolognese technique of chopping the meat—or, in this case, shellfish—finely, but then it departs from the classic. Instead of tossing the sauce with pasta, try it as a lasagne filling or serve it underneath a fillet of sautéed whitefish.

Trenne look a lot like penne, but the tubes are triangular instead of round. You might find the shape in a store specializing in Italian food products; if not, substitute penne or another short pasta.

1½ pounds jumbo shrimp in the shell

6 tablespoons extra-virgin olive oil

1 tablespoon chopped garlic

½ cup fresh basil leaves, each torn into 2 or 3 pieces

¼ to ½ teaspoon red pepper flakes, to taste

Sea salt, preferably gray salt, and freshly ground black pepper

½ cup dry white wine

½ cup Marinara Sauce (page 33)

1 tablespoon finely chopped fresh Italian (flat-leaf) parsley

1 tablespoon unsalted butter

¾ pound *trenne*, penne, or other dried short pasta

Peel and devein the shrimp, reserving the shells. Chop the shrimp finely. Put the shells in a saucepan with enough water just to cover them. Bring to a simmer, adjust the heat to maintain a simmer, and cook for 15 minutes. Strain and discard the solids. Reserve the broth.

Bring a large pot of salted water to a boil over high heat.

Meanwhile, heat the olive oil in a large skillet over high heat until hot. Add the garlic and sauté until lightly browned. Add the basil and the red pepper flakes and allow them to crackle in the hot oil for about 15 seconds.

Add the shrimp, season with salt and pepper, and stir for about 1 minute. Add the white wine and simmer until the wine is reduced by half. Add the Marinara Sauce and ¾ cup of the reserved shrimp broth and simmer for another minute. Taste and adjust the seasoning, then stir in the parsley and the butter. The sauce should be brothy, as the pasta will absorb some of the liquid. Keep the sauce warm over low heat while you cook the pasta.

Add the pasta to the boiling water and cook until it is just shy of al dente, then drain and return to the warm pot over moderate heat. Add the sauce and cook briefly so the pasta absorbs some of the sauce. Serve immediately in warmed bowls.

SERVES 4 TO 6

TAGLIATELLE WITH CHICKEN BOLOGNESE—Much leaner than the classic *ragù bolognese*, my quick chicken Bolognese gets its character from generous amounts of garlic and herbs and more subtle notes of tomato and porcini. The porcini soaking liquid also helps make the dish richer and earthier. You can make this sauce with chicken or turkey and serve it on fresh or dried pasta; my preference is for a long noodle, like fresh tagliatelle. Because the meat is finely ground, some of it may fall to the bottom of the pot as you serve the pasta. Just spoon any bits over the top.

¼ ounce dried porcini

1 cup warm water

5 tablespoons extra-virgin olive oil

¾ cup chopped onion

1½ tablespoons chopped garlic

1½ tablespoons chopped fresh Italian (flat-leaf) parsley

2 teaspoons minced fresh thyme

1 pound ground chicken or turkey

Sea salt, preferably gray salt, and freshly ground black pepper

⅓ cup dry white wine

1 cup Chicken Stock (page 22) or canned low-sodium chicken broth

¾ cup Marinara Sauce (page 33) or tomato puree
   (see Tomatoes, page 19)

1 pound fresh tagliatelle or dried spaghetti

¼ cup freshly grated Parmesan cheese, plus more for serving

In a small bowl, rehydrate the porcini in the warm water for 30 minutes. Lift the porcini out with a slotted spoon and chop finely. Strain the liquid through a double thickness of damp paper towels to catch any grit. Reserve the porcini and liquid separately.

Bring a large pot of salted water to a boil over high heat.

Meanwhile, heat the olive oil in a large skillet over moderate heat. Add the onion and sauté gently until softened, about 5 minutes; do not let it color. Add the garlic, parsley, and thyme and cook for a minute or two to release their fragrance.

Raise the heat to moderately high, add the chicken, and cook, breaking the meat up with a wooden spoon, until it loses its pinkness. Season with salt and pepper. Add the wine and simmer until it evaporates. Add the stock, ½ cup of the porcini liquid, and the porcini. Simmer for a couple of minutes to reduce the liquid, then stir in the Marinara Sauce or tomato puree. Reduce the heat to maintain a gentle simmer and cook until the sauce is well flavored and slightly thickened, about 5 minutes. Keep warm over low heat.

Add the pasta to the boiling water and cook until it is just shy of al dente. Set aside 1 cup of the pasta water, then drain the pasta. Return the pasta to the warm pot over moderate heat. Add the sauce and cook the pasta briefly so it absorbs some of the sauce. Add the ¼ cup cheese and toss again, adding some of the reserved pasta water if the sauce appears dry.

Transfer the pasta to a warmed serving bowl and serve at once. Pass more Parmesan at the table.

SERVES 4 TO 6

Michael's Notes: Dried porcini can harbor bits of grit, so it's always a good idea to lift them out of their soaking liquid, letting any grit stay behind. Then strain the liquid through damp paper towels.

RIGATONI WITH VEGETABLE BOLOGNESE — Classically a Bolognese sauce is made with meat, but I've discovered that you can apply the same techniques to vegetables to create an equally delicious vegetarian sauce. Caramelizing the mushrooms, carrots, celery, and onion is key to building a meaty flavor. You can use the sauce on long or short pasta—I like it on rigatoni—stir it into risotto, or spoon it over polenta. The only hard part is refraining from eating it right out of the pan.

5 tablespoons extra-virgin olive oil

1½ cups minced onion

1½ cups finely minced fresh mushrooms (about ⅓ pound)

½ cup finely diced carrot

½ cup finely diced celery

2 tablespoons chopped garlic

2 tablespoons finely chopped fresh Italian (flat-leaf) parsley

2 teaspoons finely chopped fresh rosemary

1 cup Marinara Sauce (page 33) or tomato puree

   (see Tomatoes, page 19)

¼ cup dry white wine

¼ cup water

Sea salt, preferably gray salt, and freshly ground black pepper

¾ pound rigatoni or spaghetti

2 tablespoons unsalted butter

2 tablespoons freshly grated Parmesan cheese, plus more for serving

---

Bring a large pot of salted water to a boil over high heat.

Meanwhile, heat a large skillet over moderately high heat. Add 4 tablespoons of the olive oil. When the oil starts to smoke, add the onion, mushrooms, carrot, and celery and sauté until softened and beginning to caramelize, 5 to 10 minutes. Add the garlic, parsley, and rosemary and sauté for about 5 minutes to release their flavor. Add the Marinara Sauce or tomato puree, the wine, the remaining 1 tablespoon oil, and the water. Bring the sauce to a simmer, season with salt and pepper, and simmer gently for 10 minutes to blend the flavors.

Add the pasta to the boiling water and cook until it is just shy of al dente. Set aside 1 cup of the pasta water, then drain the pasta. Return the pasta to the warm pot over moderately low heat. Add the sauce and the butter and cook the pasta briefly so it absorbs some of the sauce, stirring until the butter melts and adding some of the reserved pasta water if the sauce appears dry.

Transfer the pasta to a warmed serving bowl, top with the 2 tablespoons Parmesan, and serve at once. Pass more Parmesan at the table.

SERVES 4

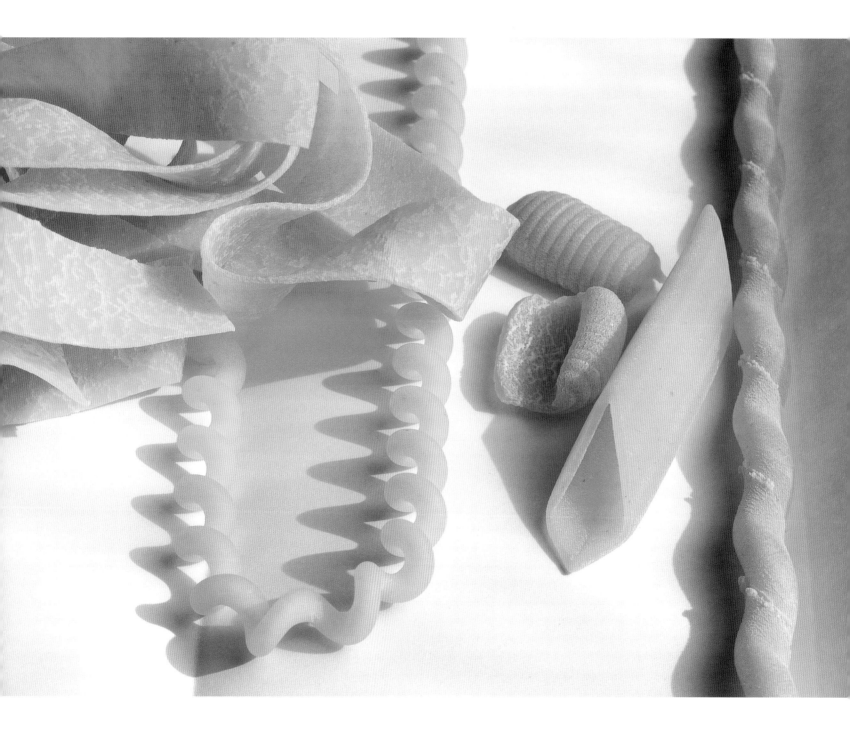

THREE PESTO POSSIBILITIES—I've always thought it would be fun to have a dinner party with a pesto bar. I'd put heaping bowls of steaming pasta on the table and let guests serve themselves to whichever pesto they preferred, or to a little of each. The following three pestos would make a good selection because they're so different in flavor—and, together, they represent the colors of *il Tricolore*, the Italian flag.

BASIL PESTO—If your pesto typically turns army green shortly after you make it, you'll appreciate the beauty of this version. I blanch the basil briefly to set the color, and I add a pinch of powdered ascorbic acid (vitamin C), which keeps the pesto from oxidizing.

2 cups firmly packed fresh basil leaves
$\frac{1}{3}$ cup olive oil
3 tablespoons pine nuts, toasted
$\frac{1}{2}$ teaspoon minced garlic
Sea salt, preferably gray salt
Powdered ascorbic acid (vitamin C)
$\frac{1}{4}$ cup freshly grated Parmesan cheese

Prepare a bowl of ice water. Bring a saucepan of water to a boil. Put the basil in a sieve and plunge it into the boiling water, pushing the leaves down into the water and stirring them so they blanch evenly. Blanch for 15 seconds, then plunge the basil into the ice water to cool quickly. Drain immediately, squeeze the basil dry, and chop it roughly.

In a blender, puree the basil with the oil, pine nuts, garlic, salt to taste, and a pinch of ascorbic acid. When well blended, add the cheese and whir briefly just to mix. Transfer to a bowl and adjust the seasoning.

MAKES ABOUT ¾ CUP, ENOUGH FOR 1 POUND PASTA

PICTURED ON PAGE 107

Michael's Notes: Don't try to make this pesto in a food processor. The processor just throws it around the bowl. A blender does a much better job. Be sure to thin the pesto with some of the hot pasta water before tossing it with pasta.

WALNUT AND RICOTTA PESTO — In this version of pesto, cheese substitutes for most of the olive oil. It makes an easy, flavorful pasta sauce: just toss a generous amount with hot pasta, a spoonful of butter, and a little of the pasta cooking water to thin. You could use this pesto as a layer in lasagne or stuff it into pasta shells. Bake the stuffed shells with tomato sauce, or drizzled with butter and sprinkled with Parmesan, until hot throughout. I like to do this pesto in a mortar (you'll need a large one), but a food processor works as well.

½ cup walnuts

5 tablespoons extra-virgin olive oil

1 tablespoon minced garlic

12 large fresh basil leaves, coarsely chopped

1½ cups Homemade Ricotta (page 39) or store-bought whole-milk ricotta cheese

½ teaspoon grated lemon zest

2 tablespoons freshly grated pecorino romano cheese

Sea salt, preferably gray salt, and freshly ground black pepper

---

Preheat the oven to 350°F. Spread the walnuts on a baking sheet and toast until fragrant and lightly browned, about 10 minutes. Let cool, then chop coarsely.

Heat 2 tablespoons of the olive oil in a small skillet over moderately high heat. Add the garlic and sauté until light brown. Scrape the garlic into a mortar or food processor and add the basil and nuts. Pound to a paste or process until finely chopped. Add the ricotta, the remaining 3 tablespoons oil, and the lemon zest, and pound or process until thoroughly blended. Transfer to a bowl and stir in the pecorino cheese and salt and pepper to taste.

MAKES A GENEROUS 2 CUPS, ENOUGH FOR 1½ POUNDS PASTA

PICTURED ON PAGE 107

TOMATO PESTO — This is a great sauce for pasta salad because it's delicious at room temperature. You could also slather it on *bruschetta*, grilled fish, or chicken. Or make a brunch dish by topping a thick slice of toast with prosciutto, a poached egg, and a little of this pesto.

In summer, when you can get your hands on vine-ripe tomatoes, you don't even need to peel them. To intensify the flavor, you can add a few Oven-Dried Tomatoes (page 37). The pesto keeps for several days in a tightly sealed container in the refrigerator.

2 cups peeled, seeded, and coarsely chopped tomatoes

1 tablespoon minced garlic

15 large fresh basil leaves

¼ cup extra-virgin olive oil

2 teaspoons balsamic vinegar

Sea salt, preferably gray salt, and freshly ground black pepper

½ cup freshly grated Parmesan cheese

Combine the tomatoes, garlic, basil, olive oil, vinegar, and salt and pepper to taste in a blender and puree until smooth. Add the cheese and whir briefly just to mix. Transfer to a bowl and adjust the seasoning.

MAKES ABOUT 2 CUPS, ENOUGH FOR 1 POUND PASTA

PICTURED ON PAGE 107

SPAGHETTINI AGLIO ED OLIO—People often ask me for my favorite pasta recipe, but the answer depends on my mood and the company. If I'm alone and starving on a weeknight, I would probably make *spaghettini aglio ed olio*, which goes together quickly and is one of the most satisfying pasta dishes I know. Many Italians like it very spicy and without a speck of cheese; adjust the red pepper flakes and cheese to your own taste.

¾ pound spaghettini or spaghetti

4 tablespoons extra-virgin olive oil

3 tablespoons finely sliced garlic

½ teaspoon red pepper flakes, or to taste

Sea salt, preferably gray salt, and freshly ground black pepper

2 tablespoons finely minced fresh Italian (flat-leaf) parsley

4 tablespoons freshly grated pecorino romano cheese

Bring a large pot of salted water to a boil over high heat. Add the pasta.

While the pasta cooks, heat 2 tablespoons of the olive oil in a large skillet over moderate heat. Add the garlic and sauté until it softens and begins to brown. Add the red pepper flakes, ½ cup of the boiling pasta water, a pinch of salt, a grinding of pepper, and the parsley. Keep warm over low heat.

When the pasta is about 1 minute shy of al dente, set aside another ½ cup of the pasta water. Drain the pasta and add it to the skillet. Cook over high heat, tossing with tongs, until the pasta absorbs most of the liquid, then add the remaining 2 tablespoons olive oil, 2 tablespoons of the pecorino, and enough of the reserved pasta water to moisten the noodles.

Transfer the pasta to a warmed serving bowl and top with the remaining 2 tablespoons pecorino. Serve immediately.

SERVES 4

Michael's Notes: I like to accentuate the flavor of the garlic by letting it caramelize lightly. To help it cook evenly when there's not a lot of oil in the skillet, I'll tip the skillet so the oil gathers on one side and let the garlic fry in that little pool.

SPAGHETTI ALL'AMATRICIANA—From Amatrice, a town near Rome, this quick pasta dish is a working person's supper. If you keep your kitchen stocked with pancetta, canned tomatoes, pasta, onions, and pecorino, you can have dinner ready in minutes.

⅓ pound pancetta in one piece, partially frozen

2 tablespoons extra-virgin olive oil

1 onion, thinly sliced onion-soup style (see Michael's Notes, page 78)

¾ pound spaghetti or *bucatini*

Scant ¼ teaspoon red pepper flakes

1 tablespoon chopped fresh Italian (flat-leaf) parsley

1½ tablespoons red wine vinegar

¾ cup tomato puree (see Tomatoes, page 19)

Freshly grated pecorino romano cheese

Bring a large pot of salted water to a boil over high heat.

Meanwhile, unroll the pancetta. Cut it into 1-inch-long chunks, then slice each chunk thinly across the grain.

Heat the olive oil in a large skillet over moderately low heat. Add the pancetta and cook until it renders some of its fat, about 5 minutes. Do not allow it to crisp. Add the onion and cook until soft, about 10 minutes. While the onion is cooking, add the pasta to the boiling water.

Add the red pepper flakes and parsley to the onion mixture and cook briefly to release their fragrance. Add the wine vinegar and simmer briskly until it evaporates, then add the tomato puree and ¼ cup of the pasta water. Simmer briefly to blend.

When the pasta is just shy of al dente, drain it and return it to the warm pot over moderate heat. Add the sauce and cook briefly so the pasta absorbs some of the sauce, then transfer to a warmed serving bowl and shower with the pecorino. Serve immediately.

SERVES 4

PICTURED RIGHT

Michael's Notes: Start boiling the pasta after the onion has softened so that you have some starchy pasta water for your sauce. Freeze the pancetta for about 30 minutes to make it easier to slice.

clam up

Clams can be sandy. Scrub them well to
keep your sauce from being gritty.

LINGUINE WITH CLAMS AND *BAGNA CAUDA* BUTTER — This dish came about because I had *Bagna Cauda* Butter in the freezer. Melted into the pasta and clams at the last minute, the butter delivers subtle notes of anchovy and garlic. I predict this sauce will turn you away from old-fashioned white clam sauce forever.

¾ pound dried linguine

2 tablespoons olive oil

4 pounds clams, scrubbed

1½ cups dry white wine

½ cup *Bagna Cauda* Butter (page 30), at room temperature

1 cup coarsely chopped fresh Italian (flat-leaf) parsley

Bring a large pot of salted water to a boil over high heat. Add the pasta.

While the pasta cooks, prepare the clams: Heat a large pot over high heat. When very hot, add the olive oil, then add the clams. When the first clams start to open, add the wine and bring to a boil. Boil for a couple of minutes to drive off the alcohol, then cover and cook until the clams open, about 5 minutes. Discard any clams that fail to open.

Drain the pasta when it is 1 minute shy of al dente and transfer it to the pot with the clams. Cook over moderate heat for about 1 minute so the pasta absorbs some of the sauce. Off the heat, add the butter and parsley and toss until the butter melts. Divide among warmed bowls and serve immediately.

SERVES 4

PICTURED LEFT

Michael's Notes: If you start the clams in a very hot skillet, they'll open twice as fast.

PASTA POMODORINI — Cherry tomatoes have a way of multiplying in the garden when your back is turned. The more you pick, the more there are. When my kids and I tire of eating them out of hand, like candy, I make a pasta sauce with them. It's especially pretty if you have red and gold varieties.

¾ pound spaghettini or spaghetti

¼ cup extra-virgin olive oil, plus more for drizzling

¼ cup sliced garlic

½ teaspoon finely minced Calabrian chilies (see Resources, page 210), or ¼ teaspoon red pepper flakes

1 pint small cherry tomatoes, stems removed, crushed between your thumb and forefinger

Sea salt, preferably gray salt

½ cup fresh basil leaves, each torn into 2 or 3 pieces

Wedge of Parmesan cheese

Bring a large pot of salted water to a boil over high heat. Add the pasta.

While the pasta cooks, heat the ¼ cup olive oil in a large skillet over moderate heat. Add the garlic and cook until the slivers are golden brown and crisp, then add the chilies and cook for about 30 seconds. Raise the heat to high and add the tomatoes. Simmer briskly to soften the tomatoes and thicken the juices, about 3 minutes. Season with salt.

When the pasta is al dente, scoop out about ½ cup of the pasta cooking water, then drain the pasta. Return the pasta to the warm pot off the heat. Add the sauce and the basil and mix well. Add some of the reserved cooking water if the pasta seems dry. Transfer to a warmed serving bowl and grate Parmesan over the top to taste. Drizzle with a little more olive oil. Serve immediately.

SERVES 4

Michael's Notes: Get your kids involved in the kitchen. Their little hands are perfect for crushing cherry tomatoes. Show them how to squish the tomatoes slowly and carefully between thumb and forefinger so the juice doesn't end up on the ceiling.

PASTINA RISOTTO WITH *SALSA ROSA* — If you are the child of Italian parents, as I am, *pastina* (small pasta) was the first pasta you learned to eat as a kid. It's like pasta with training wheels, and it comes in many shapes. Some resemble tiny tubes, grains of rice, melon seeds, or peppercorns, but they are always small and usually served floating in broth.

When I was the chef at Tra Vigne in St. Helena, I created a risotto made with *pastina* as a lighter, hot-weather alternative to the classic rice dish. Customers loved it. I parboil the pasta first, then finish cooking it by the risotto method, adding the liquid a little at a time. It turns creamy like regular risotto, but it's not as heavy. Using *Salsa Rosa* for part of the liquid gives it a gorgeous color and summery flavor.

1 pound *acini di pepe*, *rosmarino*, or other small pasta shape
Olive oil

2 tablespoons extra-virgin olive oil

2 tablespoons minced garlic

2 tablespoons chopped fresh oregano

1 cup Chicken Stock (page 22) or canned low-sodium chicken broth

1 teaspoon sea salt, preferably gray salt

6 cups firmly packed spinach leaves, large stems removed, torn

1½ cups *Salsa Rosa* (page 34)

½ cup freshly grated Parmesan cheese

Bring a large pot of salted water to a boil over high heat. Add the pasta and cook until half done. It should still have considerable firmness in the center, as it will cook more later. Set aside about 2 cups of the pasta water, then drain the pasta, rinse with cold water, and drain again. Drizzle with the olive oil to keep the pasta from sticking together. You can prepare the pasta to this point up to 8 hours ahead; refrigerate it until you are ready to finish the dish.

Heat the 2 tablespoons olive oil in a large pot over high heat. Add the garlic and sauté until browned. Add the oregano and cook briefly to release its fragrance, then add the stock or broth and salt. Bring the liquid to a boil, add the partially cooked pasta, and stir to coat. Add 1 cup of the reserved pasta water and simmer until all the liquid has been absorbed, 5 to 6 minutes.

Stir in the spinach and cook until it has wilted, then stir in the *Salsa Rosa*. Thin, if desired, with additional pasta water, then remove from the heat and stir in the Parmesan cheese. Serve at once.

SERVES 6 AS A FIRST COURSE, 8 AS A SIDE DISH

WARM PASTA SALAD WITH SPINACH AND MUSHROOMS

WARM PASTA SALAD WITH SPINACH AND MUSHROOMS — Cold pasta salads have no appeal for me, but a warm salad is something else entirely. This one has caramelized mushrooms, a splash of sherry vinegar, and spinach leaves added at the last minute to wilt in the warmth of the dish.

1 pound mixed fresh shiitake and oyster mushrooms

5 tablespoons extra-virgin olive oil

Sea salt, preferably gray salt, and freshly ground black pepper

1 tablespoon minced garlic

2 tablespoons minced fresh Italian (flat-leaf) parsley

1 tablespoon minced fresh thyme

$\frac{3}{4}$ pound penne

3 tablespoons sherry vinegar

2 cups baby spinach or coarsely torn larger spinach leaves

Wedge of Parmesan cheese

Remove the shiitake stems and cut the caps into fourths, sixths, or eighths, depending on size. By hand, break the oyster mushrooms into smaller pieces.

Heat a large skillet over high heat. Add 3 tablespoons of the olive oil. When the oil is hot, sprinkle in the mushrooms. Don't stir! Let them sizzle until they have caramelized on the bottom, about 3 minutes. If you toss them too soon, they will release their liquid and begin to steam. When the bottoms are caramelized, reduce the heat to moderately low, stir, season with salt and pepper, and continue cooking until the mushrooms are tender, about 15 minutes. Stir in the garlic, parsley, and thyme and cook for a minute or two to release their fragrance.

Meanwhile, bring a large pot of salted water to a boil over high heat. Add the pasta and cook until al dente. Drain, reserving 1 cup of the pasta water, and transfer the pasta to a large bowl. Add the mushrooms to the pasta. Return the mushroom skillet to high heat, add the reserved pasta water, and cook, stirring to scrape up any stuck-on bits, until the liquid is reduced by half. Still on the heat, whisk in the sherry vinegar, then slowly whisk in the remaining 2 tablespoons oil.

Add the contents of the skillet to the pasta and toss well. Add the spinach and toss again. Season with salt and pepper. With a vegetable peeler, shave the Parmesan over the top. Toss again gently and serve immediately.

SERVES 4

LASAGNETTE—Lasagne represents a lot of effort on the part of the cook, so guests are always impressed by it. These little lasagne (*lasagnette*, in Italian) are baked free-form; you can assemble them on a baking sheet rather than in a straight-sided casserole (although that works, too). The ricotta filling with ham and mozzarella is from Sorrento, near Naples; if you want to go all out, make your own ricotta (page 39).

FRESH TOMATO SAUCE:

1 tablespoon extra-virgin olive oil

1 clove garlic, lightly crushed

2 ½ pounds tomatoes, peeled, seeded, and pureed

1 fresh basil sprig

Sea salt, preferably gray salt

Baking soda

FILLING:

2 cups (or a 15-ounce container) ricotta cheese

2 egg yolks

2 ounces baked ham, cut into ¼-inch dice

2 ounces whole-milk mozzarella cheese, cut into ¼-inch dice

2 tablespoons freshly grated Parmesan cheese

¼ cup chopped fresh basil

Sea salt, preferably gray salt, and freshly ground black pepper

¾ pound fresh egg pasta in sheets

2 tablespoons freshly grated Parmesan cheese

2 teaspoons chopped fresh Italian (flat-leaf) parsley

Preheat the oven to 375°F.

Make the sauce: Heat the olive oil in a large skillet over moderate heat. Add the garlic and sauté until it is golden. Add the tomatoes, basil, and salt to taste and simmer until reduced to 2 cups. If the sauce tastes too tart, add a pinch of baking soda and simmer for 1 minute longer. Remove from the heat and remove the basil sprig and garlic clove.

Make the filling: In a bowl, stir to combine the ricotta, egg yolks, ham, mozzarella, Parmesan, and basil. Season with salt and pepper.

Cut the pasta sheets into 4 ½-to 5-inch squares. You will need 16 squares. Bring a large pot of salted water to a boil. Working in batches, add the pasta squares and cook until about half done, about 1 minute, then use tongs or a skimmer to transfer the sheets to ice water to cool quickly. Lift the sheets out of the ice water and place them on clean dish towels.

Lightly oil a rimmed baking sheet or large baking dish. Put ½ cup of the tomato sauce at one end of the baking sheet and spread it into the shape of a pasta square. Top the sauce with 1 pasta square, spread a scant 3 tablespoons filling evenly on the pasta, then continue making layers of pasta and filling until you have 8 layers of pasta alternating with 7 layers of filling. Spoon ½ cup of the tomato sauce on top of the last pasta layer, then sprinkle 1 tablespoon Parmesan and 1 teaspoon chopped parsley over the top. Repeat with the remaining ingredients to make 2 identical stacks.

Bake until bubbling and lightly browned, about 30 minutes. Let rest for 5 minutes, then cut each lasagne in half to make a total of 4 *lasagnette*. Serve immediately.

SERVES 4

Michael's Notes: Once you've made this lasagne my way, you can make it your own by adding components you like: maybe sautéed mushrooms or cooked spinach, goat cheese, crumbled sausage, or sliced Fontina. In winter, I use canned tomatoes for the sauce but enhance it with dried porcini.

rice, beans & polenta

A pantry stocked with rice, dried beans, canned chickpeas, and polenta is fundamental to Italian-style meals. In spring, when the first tender green vegetables appear, I'm always inclined to reach for some rice and make *Insalata di Riso* (page 120). *Risotto Bianco* (page 121) is a standby at my house, either left unadorned or paired with Shrimp Bolognese (page 103) or *Brodetto di Mare* (page 145). In winter, I'll braise white beans *all'uccelletto* (page 124) to accompany lamb, or I'll batter and fry them crisp in chili-laced oil (page 125). Raised on polenta, I love it still, served soft and creamy with ribbons of spinach and basil-flavored oil (page 129).

INSALATA DI RISO—When all my favorite spring vegetables hit the market at the same time, I start thinking about rice salad. This one's a beauty: pearly white rice, bits of pink ham, and lots of spring-green fava beans, peas, and asparagus. I like it for lunch, all by itself, but I'd also pair it with grilled shrimp or with poached salmon with tarragon mayonnaise.

You can blanch all the vegetables and cook the rice ahead, but don't dress the salad until just before serving.

1 cup Arborio rice

½ pound medium asparagus

1 cup shelled English peas (about 1 pound unshelled peas)

2 pounds fresh fava beans

2 tablespoons plus 2 teaspoons fresh lemon juice

½ cup extra-virgin olive oil

Sea salt, preferably gray salt, and freshly ground black pepper

½ cup thinly sliced fresh basil leaves

2 tablespoons chopped fresh Italian (flat-leaf) parsley

1 tablespoon grated lemon zest

½ cup diced boiled ham

¼ cup freshly grated pecorino romano cheese

Bring a large pot of salted water to a boil. Add the rice, stir, and adjust the heat to maintain a simmer. Cook, stirring occasionally to prevent any grains from sticking to the pot, until the rice is just barely done, about 15 minutes. It will continue to cook as it cools. Drain the rice well and spread it out on a tray to cool quickly.

Bring another large pot of salted water to a boil. Holding an asparagus spear in both hands, bend the spear until it breaks naturally at the point where the spear becomes tough. Discard the tough end and repeat with the remaining spears. Cut the asparagus into ⅓-inch lengths. Blanch the asparagus in the boiling water for 1 minute, then lift out with a skimmer and transfer to ice water. When cool, drain well.

Blanch the peas in the same water until just tender, 2 to 3 minutes, then lift them out with a skimmer and transfer to ice water. When cool, drain well.

Shell the fava beans, then blanch the unpeeled beans in the same boiling water for about 2 minutes. Drain and transfer them to ice water. When cool, drain again. Peel the fava beans by pinching open the loose skin; the peeled bean should slip out easily.

Put the lemon juice in a small bowl. Gradually whisk in the olive oil, then season the dressing with salt and pepper.

In a large bowl, combine the cooled rice, asparagus, peas, fava beans, basil, parsley, lemon zest, ham, and pecorino. Mix gently with your hands. Pour enough of the dressing over the salad to coat it lightly—you may not need it all—and mix again with your hands. Taste, adjust the seasoning, and serve.

SERVES 8

PICTURED ON PAGE 122

RISOTTO BIANCO — For me, making risotto is more like meditating than cooking. The twenty minutes of constant stirring allows me to slow down and reflect on my day. Although many restaurant cooks partially precook risotto to shave a few minutes off the cooking time during service, I relish the chance to make an unhurried risotto when I'm at home.

Take time to sweat the onions properly. They are the flavor foundation that the risotto rests upon. Adding salt to them encourages them to throw water, so they braise in their own juices.

About 6 cups Chicken Stock (page 22), or 3 cups canned low-sodium
    chicken broth mixed with 3 cups water

2 tablespoons extra-virgin olive oil

1 cup minced onion

1 tablespoon minced garlic

1 teaspoon sea salt, preferably gray salt

2 cups Arborio rice

½ cup dry white wine

2 tablespoons unsalted butter

¼ cup freshly grated Parmesan cheese

Freshly ground black pepper

Pour the stock or diluted broth into a saucepan and bring to a bare simmer.

Heat the olive oil in a large saucepan over moderate heat. Add the onion, garlic, and salt and sauté until the onion is soft, about 8 minutes; do not let it color. Stir in the rice and cook, stirring, until the rice is hot, about 2 minutes. Add the wine and simmer, stirring, until absorbed. Begin adding the hot stock 1 cup at a time, stirring often and adding more liquid only when the previous addition has been absorbed. Adjust the heat to maintain a simmer. It should

take about 20 minutes for the rice to become creamy and al dente. You may not need all the liquid; if you need a little more, use boiling water.

Remove the risotto from the heat and stir in the butter and Parmesan. Season with salt and pepper and divide among warmed bowls. Serve immediately.

SERVES 4

PICTURED ON PAGE 123

Michael's Notes: My own version of an ice cream social is a risotto bar. I'll make *Risotto Bianco* and then put out three or four condiments that my guests can stir in as they like, such as *Salsa Rosa* (page 34), Basil Pesto (page 108), Tomato Pesto (page 109), or any of the Bolognese sauces (pages 102–105). And nobody says they can't have some of each.

FAGIOLI ALL'UCCELLETTO— In Italian, an *uccelletto* is a small bird, so to cook beans *all'uccelletto* means to use the same seasonings you would use for a small game bird, namely, tomato, garlic, and sage. Beans prepared this way are a beloved staple in Tuscany, and it's easy to see why. They're tender and meaty and loaded with flavor, and they taste even better the second day. Serve the beans with lamb or pork, or sit down to a big bowl of them on their own when you're in the mood for a vegetarian meal.

PRECOOKED BEANS:

1 ½ cups dried cannellini beans or other large white beans

½ onion

1 celery rib, quartered

1 carrot, quartered

1 clove garlic, peeled and lightly crushed

1 bay leaf

Sea salt, preferably gray salt

¾ cup tomato puree (see Tomatoes, page 19)

2 cloves garlic, peeled and lightly crushed

3 fresh sage leaves

4 tablespoons extra-virgin olive oil

Freshly ground black pepper

Precook the beans: Place the beans in a saucepan and add cold water to cover by 2 inches. Bring to a boil, cover, and remove from the heat. Let stand for 1 hour, then drain.

Return the beans to the saucepan along with the onion, celery, carrot, garlic, and bay leaf. Add water to cover by 2 inches. Slowly bring to a simmer over moderately low heat. (If you heat them too fast, the skins may break.) Adjust the heat to maintain a bare simmer and cook, uncovered, until the beans are almost tender, 20 minutes or longer, depending on the age of the beans. Add salt to taste and continue cooking until the beans are tender but not mushy. Remove from the heat and let cool in the liquid. (You can prepare the beans to this point 1 to 2 days ahead; cover and refrigerate.)

Preheat the oven to 400°F. Drain the beans and discard the vegetables but reserve the liquid. In a casserole that can go from the stove top to the oven, combine the beans, 1 ½ cups of the bean liquid, the tomato puree, garlic, sage, and 3 tablespoons of the olive oil. Season with salt and pepper. Bring to a simmer on top of the stove, then transfer to the oven and bake, uncovered, at a gentle simmer (adjust oven temperature if necessary) until the beans have absorbed the liquid, 45 minutes or more.

Remove from the oven and let rest for 15 to 20 minutes, then stir in the remaining 1 tablespoon olive oil, taste for seasoning, and serve.

SERVES 6

Michael's Notes: When the recipe calls for swirling in 1 tablespoon olive oil at the end, that's the moment to get out your best extra-virgin olive oil.

CRISPY WHITE BEANS WITH CHILI OIL — This dish, now a personal favorite, was a total mistake. One day I was sautéing some white beans, got caught up in something else, and when I looked at the beans again, they were overcooked. I spooned them onto a paper towel and, a few minutes later, popped one in my mouth. To my surprise, I couldn't stop eating them.

I've worked on the recipe a bit to create something that's now intentionally crisp and delicious. You could put these beans out with cocktails as a crunchy nibble, like peanuts, but I typically serve them as a side dish for lobster or shrimp.

BEANS:

1 cup dried white beans, preferably the largest available

2 fresh sage leaves

1 clove garlic, peeled but left whole

2 teaspoons sea salt, preferably gray salt

COATING:

1 cup Arborio Rice Coating (page 24)

1½ teaspoons pure California chili powder (see Resources, page 210)

¼ teaspoon freshly ground black pepper

¾ cup buttermilk

¾ cup plus 2 tablespoons extra-virgin olive oil

¼ cup Chili Oil (page 32)

2 tablespoons thinly sliced garlic

1 tablespoon thinly sliced serrano or jalapeño chili

1½ cups fresh basil leaves

1 tablespoon julienned orange zest

Cook the beans: Place the dried beans in a saucepan with cold water to cover by 2 inches. Bring to a boil. Cover, remove from the heat, and let stand for 1 hour. Drain the beans, return to the saucepan, and add cold water to cover by 2 inches, the sage, and the garlic. Slowly bring to a simmer. Simmer gently, uncovered, for about 20 minutes, then add the salt. Continue simmering gently until the beans are tender; the timing will vary depending on the age of the beans. Let cool in the cooking liquid. (The beans may be refrigerated for up to 3 days before continuing.)

Make the coating: Combine the rice coating, chili powder, and pepper in a small bowl, stir well, and set aside.

Drain the beans through a sieve and discard the sage and garlic. Place the beans in a bowl, add the buttermilk, and let soak for a few minutes. Drain again in a sieve, then place the sieve with the beans over a bowl.

Heat the ¾ cup olive oil and the Chili Oil in a medium skillet over high heat. While the oil is heating, sprinkle the coating over the beans and shake in the sieve to coat the beans evenly. Repeat with the coating that falls into the bowl. Don't worry if the beans don't absorb all the coating.

When the oil is hot but not smoking, carefully add the beans, spreading them in an even layer. Cook without stirring until they are browned and crisp on the bottom, 6 to 7 minutes. Turn with a spatula and brown on the other side, another 5 to 6 minutes, adjusting the heat so they don't burn. With a slotted spoon, transfer the beans to paper towels to drain.

Pour off the oil from the skillet and wipe it clean with paper towels. Return the skillet to moderately high heat and add the remaining 2 tablespoons oil. When hot, add the sliced garlic and chili and sauté until the garlic begins to color. Add the basil leaves and stand back; they will spatter. Sauté until the leaves turn crisp, about 1 minute. Add the orange zest, then remove from the heat.

Arrange the beans on a serving platter and top with the garlic-chili-basil garnish. Serve hot.

SERVES 4

PICTURED ON FOLLOWING PAGE

Michael's Notes: Bringing the beans up to a simmer slowly helps keep the skins from splitting.

hot stuff

The Aborio Rice Coating makes the beans extra crunchy when fried.

CENTER: CRISPY WHITE BEANS WITH CHILI OIL, PAGE 125; RIGHT: DAMN HOT POLENTA BREAD, PAGE 128

DAMN HOT POLENTA BREAD—Don't pass this recipe by thinking it might be too spicy. Despite the name, it isn't that hot. The Damn Hot Peppers give it only a little warmth—just enough to make you realize this isn't your grandmother's corn bread. It's fantastic with barbecued ribs (page 162) or chicken. When it's stale, I use it in stuffings for game birds or turkey, and I bet it would make great *panzanella* (bread salad).

You'll need finely ground polenta for this bread (I like Beretta brand). Some polentas are too coarse, and cornmeal is too fine. Take a close look at the grain if you're buying it from a bulk bin. It should be coarser than cornmeal but not gritty. Don't buy quick-cooking polenta, which has been precooked, then dried.

Unsalted butter

2 cups unbleached all-purpose flour

1 ½ cups fine polenta (see introduction to Soft Polenta
    with Greens and Basil Oil, page 129)

1 cup grated Asiago cheese

⅓ cup finely sliced green onion tops

¼ cup sugar

2 tablespoons baking powder

2 teaspoons baking soda

1 ½ teaspoons sea salt, preferably gray salt

4 extra-large eggs, lightly beaten

1 ½ cups buttermilk

½ cup finely minced Damn Hot Peppers (page 37)

½ cup salted butter, melted

Preheat the oven to 350°F. Generously butter a 9-by-13-inch baking dish.

In a large bowl, stir to combine the flour, polenta, cheese, green onion tops, sugar, baking powder, baking soda, and salt. In another bowl, whisk together the eggs, buttermilk, Damn Hot Peppers, and melted butter. Add the liquid ingredients to the dry ingredients and stir with a rubber spatula just until blended; do not overmix.

Transfer the batter to the prepared dish and level it with a rubber spatula. Bake until the bread is golden brown and firm to the touch, about 35 minutes. Cool briefly, then cut into squares and serve warm.

SERVES 12

PICTURED ON PRECEDING PAGE

Michael's Notes: Whipped honey butter is wonderful on this warm quick bread. To make it, beat softened butter in a mixer until creamy, then beat in honey and cracked black pepper to taste.

SOFT POLENTA WITH GREENS AND BASIL OIL — In southern Italy, where my parents were born, polenta is used like pasta to help feed a large family affordably. Even though it's peasant food, eating it is one of life's great pleasures. To me, polenta feels as warm and comforting as a hug.

I prefer Italian polenta, such as Beretta brand, because it tends to be ground finer than domestic polenta. The finer grind gives the finished polenta the proper creamy texture without any grittiness.

4½ cups water

Sea salt, preferably gray salt

1 cup fine polenta

1½ tablespoons freshly grated Parmesan cheese

1 tablespoon Basil Oil (page 31), plus 4 teaspoons for garnish

2 cups firmly packed spinach leaves, cut into ½-inch-wide ribbons,
   or 2 cups baby spinach

1 to 2 tablespoons unsalted butter

Bring the water to a boil in a large pot. Salt it well, then add the polenta gradually, whisking constantly. When the mixture thickens, switch to a wooden spoon and adjust the heat to maintain a bare simmer. Cook, stirring often, until thick, smooth, and creamy, about 40 minutes. Season to taste with salt.

Stir in the Parmesan and the 1 tablespoon Basil Oil. Stir in the spinach and cook until it wilts, about 1 minute. Remove from the heat and stir in the butter. Divide the polenta among 4 warmed bowls. Drizzle each portion with 1 teaspoon Basil Oil. Serve immediately.

SERVES 4

Michael's Notes: Think of polenta not as a recipe but as a ratio. For creamy polenta like this one, plan on 4½ parts liquid to 1 part polenta. You can substitute other liquids, such as chicken or vegetable stock, for the water, or add some roasted red pepper puree. Just remember to consider the puree as part of the liquid.

Variation: One of my favorite ways to serve polenta is to spread the polenta on a board or piece of wax paper. Everyone marks off a section of polenta and tops it with a favorite topping, such as marinara sauce (page 33).

SOFT POLENTA VARIATION (PAGE 129) TOPPED WITH MARINARA (PAGE 33), PARMESAN, AND BASIL

fish & shellfish

I know many Americans order fish and shellfish in restaurants but are reluctant to cook it at home. Perhaps they fear it because it can be expensive, or because they've bought seafood in the past that wasn't fresh. I hope these recipes will convert some home cooks because eating seafood is so good for our health.

My family had modest means and I grew up eating the least expensive catch of the sea, such as anchovies and sardines. I still love those tiny fish, but over many years as a restaurant chef, I've developed favorite ways to prepare the varieties that my customers were more comfortable eating, such as salmon, shrimp, and sole. Some of these recipes, like Shrimp Boil (page 146) and Planked Salmon with Basil-Chive Butter (page 144), are great for entertaining; others, such as Baked Swordfish with *Salsa Puttanesca* and Basil Oil (page 139), make easy weeknight meals.

Seek out a good fishmonger and treat yourself to fresh seafood at least once a week. Remember that most commercial fishermen take weekends off, so avoid buying fish on Sunday or Monday.

GRILLED TUNA *TONNATO* — I love classic Italian dishes like *vitello tonnato*—cold roast veal with tuna sauce—but sometimes it's fun to give the classics a whimsical twist. My tuna-sauced tuna is not only a play on words, but a great dish for entertaining. You can make the sauce ahead, and even grill the tuna before guests arrive, and serve it at room temperature.

You'll need high-quality imported olive oil–packed tuna for the sauce. Look for Portuguese and Italian brands. I drain off the oil in the can because it's usually of inferior quality, and then replace it with extra-virgin oil. You'll also need caper berries, which are the fruit of the caper bush. The capers themselves are the unopened flower buds.

SAUCE:

1 can (7 ounces or 200 grams) imported olive oil–packed tuna, drained

¼ cup extra-virgin olive oil

5 caper berries, stemmed, or 2 heaping teaspoons capers

1 tablespoon brine from the caper berries or capers

1½ teaspoons minced fresh Italian (flat-leaf) parsley

¼ teaspoon freshly ground black pepper

1½ teaspoons fresh lemon juice, or more to taste

¼ cup water, or as needed

Sea salt, preferably gray salt

1 teaspoon coriander seed

4 tuna steaks, each 6 ounces and about ¾ inch thick

Extra-virgin olive oil

Sea salt, preferably gray salt, and freshly ground black pepper

SALAD:

2 tomatoes, cut into 1-inch dice

½ medium red onion, sliced onion-soup style
   (see Michael's Notes, page 78)

16 caper berries, stemmed and sliced, or 2 tablespoons rinsed and
   chopped capers

5-inch piece English cucumber, peeled, halved lengthwise, seeded,
   and sliced on the diagonal ⅛ inch thick

⅔ cup fresh Italian (flat-leaf) parsley leaves

3 to 4 tablespoons extra-virgin olive oil

½ lemon

Sea salt, preferably gray salt, and freshly ground black pepper

---

Make the sauce: Put the tuna, olive oil, caper berries or capers, caper brine, parsley, pepper, 1½ teaspoons lemon juice, and ¼ cup water in a blender. Blend until smooth. Add a little more water if needed to make a puree. Transfer to a bowl. Season with salt and add a little more lemon juice if needed.

Prepare a hot charcoal fire in a grill, preheat a gas grill, or preheat a stove-top griddle until very hot.

Toast the coriander seed in a small skillet over moderately low heat until fragrant. Let cool, then pound to a powder in a mortar. Brush the tuna with olive oil, then season with salt, pepper, and the ground coriander.

Make the salad: Combine the tomatoes, onion, caper berries or capers, cucumber, and parsley leaves in a large bowl. Set aside.

Grill tuna to desired doneness. I like it rare, which takes about 1½ minutes per side over a hot charcoal fire.

Put about ¼ cup sauce on each of 4 dinner plates. Top each with a tuna steak.

To finish the salad, add the olive oil, a squeeze of lemon, and salt and pepper to taste. Toss, taste, and adjust the seasoning. Mound the salad on top of the tuna, dividing it evenly and leaving any juice behind in the bowl. Serve immediately.

SERVES 4

Michael's Notes: You can also use the tuna sauce on tomato salads, on steamed vegetables, or as a dip for crudités. I've even tossed it with pasta.

SOLE AMANDINE À LA TURLOCK—When I was a young, novice cook in Turlock, California, the guys from the Blue Diamond almond cooperative used to come into the restaurant where I worked. I would make this dish for them, using abalone and California smoked almonds, and I fondly remember it as one of my first successes as a professional cook. The preparation works well with sole, and with swordfish, too.

2 pounds skinless sole fillets

Sea salt, preferably gray salt, and freshly ground black pepper

½ cup Arborio Rice Coating (page 24) or Wondra flour

2 tablespoons olive oil

6 tablespoons unsalted butter

½ cup golden raisins, soaked in hot water for 20 minutes, then drained

¼ cup dry white wine

2 tablespoons fresh lemon juice

2 tablespoons minced fresh Italian (flat-leaf) parsley

½ cup whole smoked almonds, chopped in half

Put a serving platter in a low oven to warm. Season the sole with salt and pepper. Put the rice coating or flour on a plate and lightly dredge the fillets on one side only (not the skinned side); shake off any excess.

Heat 2 large skillets over moderately high heat. Put 1 tablespoon olive oil in each skillet and swirl to coat. Add the fish, coated-side down. Cook for about 1 minute, then add 1 tablespoon butter to each skillet. Continue cooking the fish until it begins to turn opaque around the edges, about 3 minutes longer. With a long spatula, turn the fillets out onto the warmed serving platter, browned-side up.

Set one of the skillets aside. Pour off any fat in the other skillet and return it to moderate heat. Add the remaining 4 tablespoons butter and cook until it turns nut brown and fragrant. Add the raisins, wine, and lemon juice. Simmer briefly to evaporate the alcohol in the wine.

Remove from the heat and stir in the parsley and almonds. Spoon the sauce over the fish. Serve immediately.

SERVES 4

Michael's Notes: I cook the sole on one side only because it's such a delicate fish. I think it's better to get one side nice and caramelized than to try to cook both sides. If you put the fillets on a heated plate, they will cook through completely.

SLOW-ROASTED HALIBUT WITH ASPARAGUS AND *SALSA GENOVESE* — This is what I call a Tuesday dish, a really simple but satisfying recipe that gets dinner on the table in twenty minutes. Baking the halibut in a low oven gives it an exceptionally moist texture, and it's a technique you can use on salmon and other fish fillets. I think you'll like the asparagus technique, too. It takes a few minutes to slice them, but then they're cooked quickly with no added water, so they're never soggy.

1 pound thick asparagus

2 ½ tablespoons extra-virgin olive oil

4 halibut fillets, about 6 ounces each, skinned

Sea salt, preferably gray salt, and freshly ground black pepper

2 tablespoons dry white wine

1 tablespoon unsalted butter

3 tablespoons *Salsa Genovese* (page 33) mixed with

    1 tablespoon extra-virgin olive oil

Holding an asparagus spear in both hands, bend the spear gently. It will break naturally at the point at which it becomes tough. Discard the tough end and repeat with the remaining spears. Slice the trimmed spears on a sharp diagonal as thinly as possibly, then set aside. (I line up two at a time to make this go faster.)

Preheat the oven to 300°F. Put 1 ½ tablespoons of the olive oil in a shallow baking dish. Place the fish fillets in the baking dish and turn to coat them with the oil. Season with salt and pepper. Spoon the wine around the fish. Bake until the fish just flakes, about 20 minutes.

About 5 minutes before the fish is ready, heat the remaining 1 tablespoon olive oil and the butter in a large skillet over moderately high heat. Add the asparagus, season with salt and pepper, and sauté until just tender, about 4 minutes.

Make a mound of asparagus in the center of each of 4 warmed plates. Use an offset spatula to place a halibut fillet on top of each mound of asparagus. Whisk a tablespoon or two of the juices from the baking dish into the *Salsa Genovese* and oil mixture to thin and flavor it, then spoon the sauce over the fish. Serve at once.

SERVES 4

BAKED SWORDFISH WITH *SALSA PUTTANESCA* AND BASIL OIL

BAKED SWORDFISH WITH *SALSA PUTTANESCA* AND BASIL OIL — In Italy, *salsa puttanesca* is used on pasta, but I love it on firm, meaty fish, like swordfish or tuna. It's also great on sautéed eggplant, on braised or boiled cauliflower, or on roasted veal.

Stories abound about why this piquant sauce is named for the ladies of the night. One theory is that they like it because it's quickly made, so it doesn't keep them away from clients for long.

SALSA PUTTANESCA:

1½ cups tomato puree (see Tomatoes, page 19)

¼ cup bottled clam juice, preferably unsalted

2 tablespoons chopped fresh Italian (flat-leaf) parsley

1 tablespoon chopped fresh oregano

2 teaspoons anchovy minced to a paste

2 teaspoons capers, rinsed and chopped

1½ teaspoons red wine vinegar

1½ teaspoons finely minced Calabrian chilies (see Resources, page 210),
     or red pepper flakes to taste

⅔ cup each Kalamata and Picholine olives, pitted and quartered

½ cup peeled, seeded, and finely diced tomato

4 swordfish steaks, each 6 ounces and about 1 inch thick

Sea salt, preferably gray salt, and freshly ground black pepper

2 tablespoons extra-virgin olive oil

4 teaspoons Basil Oil (page 31)

¼ cup thinly sliced fresh basil

Preheat the oven to 400°F.

Make the sauce: In a bowl, whisk together the tomato puree and clam juice. Stir in the parsley, oregano, anchovy paste, capers, red wine vinegar, chilies, olives, and tomato. Taste and adjust the seasoning. Divide the sauce in half. Refrigerate one-half for use on pasta in the next day or two. Heat the other half in a skillet over moderate heat, then adjust the heat to keep the sauce hot without simmering.

Season the swordfish with salt and pepper. Heat a large oven-proof skillet over high heat. When hot, add the olive oil. Add the swordfish, reduce the heat slightly, and cook on one side until nicely seared, about 2 minutes. Turn the steaks and transfer the skillet to the oven. Bake until the fish is done throughout (test with a fork), 3 to 4 minutes.

Transfer the swordfish to individual plates. Top each steak with some of the sauce, dividing it equally, then drizzle Basil Oil on the fish and on the plate. Garnish each steak with the basil.

SERVES 4

PICTURED ON PAGE 141

Michael's Notes: This recipe makes enough sauce for two meals. What you don't use on the swordfish, you can use on pasta a day or two later.

SEARED SEA BASS WITH ARTICHOKE SALAD — This is a two-for-one recipe. In addition to the sea bass with its beautiful salad topping, you get an artichoke recipe that you'll use again and again. You can chop the roasted artichokes and toss them with spaghetti, or you can puree them and fold them into a risotto at the end. You could also sauté a halibut fillet on one side, turn it over, top it with the roasted artichoke puree and some bread crumbs, then finish baking the fish in the oven.

ROASTED ARTICHOKES:

$\frac{1}{3}$ cup fresh lemon juice

6 medium artichokes

$\frac{2}{3}$ cup extra-virgin olive oil

3 cloves garlic, quartered lengthwise

1 teaspoon minced fresh thyme

1 bay leaf

1 teaspoon sea salt, preferably gray salt

Freshly ground black pepper

1 small red onion, thinly sliced onion-soup style
   (see Michael's Notes, page 78)

$\frac{3}{4}$ cup firmly packed fresh Italian (flat-leaf) parsley leaves

24 pitted Kalamata olives, quartered lengthwise

$\frac{1}{2}$ lemon

6 sea bass fillets, 5 to 6 ounces each, skinned

Sea salt, preferably gray salt, and freshly ground black pepper

$\frac{1}{2}$ cup Arborio Rice Coating (page 24) or Wondra flour

3 tablespoons extra-virgin olive oil

6 lemon wedges

Preheat the oven to 325°F.

Make the artichokes: Select a nonreactive bowl large enough to hold all the artichokes once they are trimmed, and pour the lemon juice into it. Working with 1 artichoke at a time, bend the tough outer leaves backward until they break at the point where the tough leaf becomes part of the tender base; stop when you reach the more tender interior leaves that are at least half yellow-green. With a serrated knife, cut across the leaves at the point where the color changes from yellow-green to dark green. Trim the stem of its outer layer, then trim the base, removing any dark green bits. Halve the artichokes lengthwise and scoop out the hairy choke. As the artichokes are trimmed, drop them into the bowl holding the lemon juice and turn to coat. Toss occasionally to keep them coated with lemon.

When all the artichokes are trimmed, transfer them and the lemon juice to a large skillet and add the olive oil, garlic, thyme, bay leaf, salt, and pepper to taste. Bring to a boil over moderate heat, tossing to coat the artichokes with the seasonings, then

transfer to the oven and cook until the artichokes are browned in spots and tender when pierced, about 35 minutes. Let cool, then cut each half into quarters or thirds lengthwise.

In a bowl, combine the artichokes, onion, parsley, and olives. Just before serving, season to taste with lemon juice, using the lemon half.

Season the fish fillets on both sides with salt and pepper. Spread the rice coating or flour on a plate and dredge the fish on both sides, shaking off the excess.

Heat 2 skillets over high heat. Divide the olive oil evenly between the skillets. When hot, add the fish, reduce the heat to moderate, and cook until nicely browned, about 5 minutes. Turn the fish and cook on the second side until the fish is done throughout (test with a fork), about 4 minutes, depending on thickness.

Transfer the fish to a serving platter or individual plates. Top each portion with some of the artichoke salad. Garnish with the lemon wedges.

SERVES 6

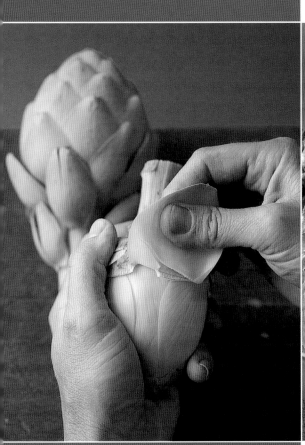

choked up

Bend the leaves back until they break at the base.

PLANKED SALMON WITH BASIL-CHIVE BUTTER

Cooking fish on a cedar plank is an old Native American technique. As the planks get hot, the aromatic oils are released and permeate the fish. You can find untreated cedar shingles or shims at lumberyards, or ask to have a 1-by-6 cut into two-foot-long lengths. Soak the planks for at least twelve hours to prevent flare-ups, weighting the boards to keep them from floating.

$^3/_4$ teaspoon sea salt, preferably gray salt

$^1/_4$ teaspoon freshly ground black pepper

$^1/_4$ teaspoon dry mustard

4 salmon fillets, 6 ounces each, skinned

1 tablespoon unsalted butter, melted

2 untreated cedar planks, each about 5 by 12 inches, soaked in water
   to cover for at least 12 hours

Extra-virgin olive oil

4 tablespoons Basil-Chive Butter (page 29), at room temperature

Preheat the broiler.

In a small bowl or cup, mix the salt, pepper, and dry mustard. Brush the top of the salmon fillets (not the skinned side) with the melted butter. Season both sides with the spice mixture.

Put the soaked planks under the hot broiler, about 5 inches from the heat source, until the wood is browned on top, about 3 minutes. With tongs, carefully remove the planks from the oven.

Immediately brush the browned surface with olive oil, then lay the salmon fillets on the oiled surface, skinned-side down. Return the planks to the broiler and cook the fish until it is done to your taste, about 6 minutes for medium.

Remove the fillets to a platter or serve directly from the planks. Top each fillet with 1 tablespoon of the Basil-Chive Butter, spreading it so that it melts evenly over the salmon. Serve immediately.

SERVES 4

TUSCAN SHRIMP WITH WHITE BEANS

Here's a dish that will benefit from that expensive Tuscan oil you've been saving. Drizzle it on these warm white beans just before you top them with sizzling shrimp, and you'll understand why great olive oil is worth its price.

2 cups cooked white beans
   (See Crispy White Beans with Chili Oil, page 125)

6 tablespoons extra-virgin olive oil

16 large shrimp, peeled (tail left on) and deveined

Sea salt, preferably gray salt

1 small serrano chili, thinly sliced

1 tablespoon sliced garlic

1 cup peeled, seeded, and diced tomato

$^1/_2$ cup fresh basil leaves

1 tablespoon fresh lemon juice

1 tablespoon chopped fresh Italian (flat-leaf) parsley

Best-quality extra-virgin olive oil

Preheat the oven to 250°F.

Put the white beans in a saucepan with just enough of their cooking liquid to moisten them. Add 2 tablespoons of the olive oil and bring the beans to a simmer. Keep them warm while you prepare the shrimp.

Heat the remaining 4 tablespoons olive oil in a large skillet over high heat. Add the shrimp, season with salt, and cook for about 1 minute, tossing frequently. Remove the shrimp with tongs to a bowl. Add the chili and garlic to the pan and sauté until the garlic browns. Add the tomato and basil, stir briefly, then add the lemon juice. Cook for about 1 minute, then stir in the parsley and the shrimp. Toss well and cook briefly to reheat the shrimp.

Spoon the white beans on a platter or individual plates. Drizzle them with the best olive oil you have, then top with the shrimp. Serve immediately.

SERVES 4

BRODETTO DI MARE — This Italian shellfish stew is one of the most popular dishes I made as a restaurant chef, and it translates easily to the home kitchen. I like to serve it over *Risotto Bianco* (page 121), but it's equally good with crusty bread, or spooned over garlic toast or over rigatoni. If you don't have a skillet large enough to accommodate the scallops and shrimp without crowding them, cook them separately, dividing the oil between them.

½ pound sea scallops

½ pound shrimp, peeled and deveined

Sea salt, preferably gray salt, and freshly ground black pepper

3 tablespoons extra-virgin olive oil

1 tablespoon minced garlic

2 tablespoons Pernod

1 cup dry white wine

¾ pound clams, scrubbed

½ pound mussels, scrubbed and debearded

2 cups peeled, seeded, and finely diced tomato

1½ tablespoons chopped fresh tarragon

2 tablespoons unsalted butter

Season the scallops and shrimp well with salt and pepper. Heat a large skillet over high heat. When hot, add 2 tablespoons of the olive oil. Add the scallops and shrimp and brown well on one side, about 2 minutes, then turn and cook about 1 minute on the second side. Transfer the shellfish to a platter and return the skillet to moderate heat.

Add the remaining 1 tablespoon oil and the garlic to the skillet over moderately high heat. Sauté until the garlic begins to color, then add the Pernod. Simmer until the Pernod evaporates, then add the wine and simmer until reduced by half.

Add the clams and mussels, cover, and raise the heat to high. Cook until they open, 3 to 5 minutes, checking occasionally and removing them to the platter as they open. Discard any that failed to open.

Add the tomato to the skillet along with any accumulated shellfish juices on the platter. Simmer for about 2 minutes to soften the tomato, then reduce the heat to moderately low and stir in the tarragon and butter. When the butter melts, return all the shellfish to the sauce and reheat briefly. Serve immediately.

SERVES 4

Michael's Notes: If you are serving the *brodetto* with the risotto, you'll want them to be ready at the same time. Start the risotto first, then start cooking the *brodetto* after you add the first liquid to the risotto.

SHRIMP BOIL—For fifteen years, a seafood boil has been my Fourth of July tradition. It is a crowd pleaser, and it is as easy to do for twenty as for two. I spread butcher paper on the tables, put a variety of hot sauces out (my favorite is Crystal brand), plus bowls of melted butter, sea salt, and Fennel Spice. When the shrimp and vegetables are ready, I dump them directly onto the table. And when everyone has finished, we roll up the butcher paper and dive into the pool to rinse off.

¼ cup fennel seed

2 tablespoons black peppercorns

2 tablespoons coriander seed

1 tablespoon red pepper flakes

2 bay leaves

6 quarts water

2 lemons, halved

1 head garlic, sliced through the equator but not all the way through

1 cup dry white wine

½ cup sea salt, preferably gray salt

8 small boiling potatoes

2 onions, unpeeled, ends removed

4 medium artichokes (no need to trim)

1 pound jumbo shrimp in the shell

GARNISHES:

Melted unsalted butter

Sea salt, preferably gray salt

Fennel Spice (page 23)

Hot-pepper sauce

Combine the fennel seed, peppercorns, coriander seed, red pepper flakes, and bay leaves and tie in a cheesecloth bag. Put the bag in a large pot with the water, the lemon halves, the garlic, the wine, and the salt. Cover and bring to a simmer, then simmer for 10 minutes.

Add the potatoes, onions, and artichokes and simmer gently, covered, until they are tender. As they are done, remove them to a serving platter. The potatoes may take 20 minutes or more; the onions and artichokes will take 30 to 40 minutes.

After you have removed all the vegetables, add the shrimp. Cook just until they turn pink, about 3 minutes. Remove them with a slotted spoon to the serving platter.

Cut the onions in half. Cut the artichokes in half and scoop out and discard the chokes.

Serve the shrimp, potatoes, onions, and artichokes with shallow bowls of melted butter, sea salt, and Fennel Spice for dipping, and with jars of hot sauce.

SERVES 4

meat & poultry

If you've taken the time to stock up on some Homemade Pantry ingredients (pages 21–39), you'll have a head start on several of these recipes. Forever-Roasted Pork with Toasted Spice Rub (page 161), Veal Milanese with *Salsa Rosa* (page 155), Grilled Lamb Steaks with Herbes de Napa (page 150), and Grilled Pork Chops with Peck Seasoning and Charred Peppers (page 160) show how you can rely on what's on the shelf or in the freezer to make your meals so much simpler.

Please treat your family to natural poultry raised without antibiotics or growth hormones. The birds may cost a little more, but I think they are an investment worth making for both health and flavor.

GRILLED LAMB STEAKS WITH HERBES DE NAPA — Lamb steaks aren't in many supermarket meat cases, so you'll need a friendly butcher in order to make this dish. But every butcher will know what you mean if you ask to have steaks cut from the top of the leg, using the band saw. It's the same cut as a ham steak, and like a ham steak, it has a bit of the leg bone in it. Grilled until crusty and medium-rare, these thick steaks make much more satisfying eating than a butterflied boneless leg of lamb. I like to serve them with undressed greens, like watercress, and let the flavorful juices from the meat dress the greens. *Fagioli all'Uccelletto* (page 124) would be another great accompaniment.

4 lamb leg steaks, each about ½ pound and ¾ to 1 inch thick

Red wine vinegar

Sea salt, preferably gray salt, and freshly ground black pepper

1½ tablespoons Herbes de Napa (page 23)

Extra-virgin olive oil

1 or 2 bunches watercress or arugula, thick stems removed, or ½ pound baby lettuces

1 lemon, quartered

Splash the lamb with the wine vinegar and rub it in gently to remove any gamy flavor. Season the lamb with salt, pepper, and Herbes de Napa, crushing the herbs between your fingers as you add them. Rub the lamb all over with olive oil. Let stand at room temperature for 1 hour.

Prepare a medium-hot charcoal fire in a grill, or preheat a gas grill. Grill the lamb steaks on both sides until medium-rare, about 3 minutes per side. Let rest for a few minutes to settle the juices, then divide the steaks among 4 dinner plates. Add a large cluster of watercress or other greens and a lemon wedge to each plate.

SERVES 4

INGREDIENTS PICTURED ON PAGE 153

Michael's Notes: If you like to cook, you can have no better friend than a good butcher. Old-fashioned butcher shops are rare these days, but you can probably find a market that has a butcher on staff and get to know him or her. When you need a special cut like these lamb steaks, it helps to have a personal relationship.

BABY LAMB CHOPS WITH ARTICHOKES AND EGG-LEMON SAUCE—You may be familiar with the Greek *avgolemono* (egg-lemon) sauce, but the same sauce is also part of Italian Jewish tradition. The egg-lemon mixture is added off the heat, and it immediately thickens the pan juices into a creamy, tangy sauce that is unforgettable.

This dish goes together quickly, so be sure you have all your ingredients prepared before you start cooking. If you can't find baby lamb chops, you can substitute chicken breasts or veal scallopini, both pounded thin.

2 eggs

1 ½ tablespoons fresh lemon juice

12 baby lamb rib chops

Sea salt, preferably gray salt, and freshly ground black pepper

½ cup unbleached all-purpose flour

4 tablespoons extra-virgin olive oil

½ cup dry white wine

½ cup Chicken Stock (page 22) or canned low-sodium broth

2 tablespoons finely minced fresh Italian (flat-leaf) parsley

1 large clove garlic, minced

½ recipe Roasted Artichokes (page 142), quarters halved lengthwise

In a small bowl, whisk together the eggs and lemon juice.

Season the chops with salt and pepper. Just before you are ready to cook, dip the chops in the flour to coat both sides lightly. Shake off the excess.

Heat a large, heavy skillet over high heat. When the skillet is very hot, add 2 tablespoons of the olive oil and swirl to coat, then add the chops. Sear them on one side until you see bloody juices rising, 3 to 4 minutes, then turn and cook for about 30 seconds on the second side. Transfer to a platter and keep warm in a low oven. Pour off the excess fat in the skillet.

Return the skillet to high heat, add the wine, and stir with a wooden spoon to release any flavorful bits stuck to the skillet. Add the stock or broth and simmer until reduced by one-third. Pour the reduced liquid into a bowl and wipe out the skillet with a paper towel.

Return the skillet to moderately high heat and add the remaining 2 tablespoons olive oil. When hot, add the parsley and garlic and sauté briefly to release their fragrance. Add the artichokes and stir to coat with the seasonings, then return the liquid to the pan. Bring to a simmer, then remove the skillet from the heat and add the egg-lemon mixture. Swirl the pan constantly until the eggs thicken the sauce, which will happen quickly.

Spoon the artichokes and sauce onto a warmed platter. Top with the lamb chops and serve immediately.

SERVES 4

Michael's Notes: It's important to use a skillet large enough to accommodate all the chops comfortably and to get it very hot before adding them, or they won't sear properly.

LEFT: HERBES DE NAPA, PAGE 23; RIGHT: GRILLED LAMB STEAKS WITH HERBES DE NAPA, PAGE 150

VEAL MILANESE WITH *SALSA ROSA* — If you think veal cutlets are a heavy dish from the past, I urge you to try these. They are truly fork-tender and wonderful with a drizzle of *Salsa Rosa*, a squeeze of lemon, and an arugula salad. I'm thrilled when I have left-over veal Milanese because it makes a terrific sandwich.

You can ask the butcher to pound the scallopini for you if you want to save time. You can also coat them a few hours before frying. Arrange the coated scallopini in a single layer on a tray and refrigerate.

I use pure olive oil, usually labeled simply "olive oil," for frying the scallopini. It has a higher smoking point and is less expensive than extra-virgin oil. If you are concerned about fat, you could fry the veal in a nonstick skillet with only a tablespoon or two of oil.

8 veal scallopini from the round (leg), about 2 ounces each
Sea salt, preferably gray salt, and freshly ground black pepper

COATING:
1½ cups Fine Dried Bread Crumbs (page 38)
½ cup freshly grated Parmesan cheese
2 tablespoons minced fresh Italian (flat-leaf) parsley
1 teaspoon sea salt, preferably gray salt
Freshly ground black pepper
1 tablespoon olive oil
½ cup unbleached all-purpose flour
2 eggs

Olive oil for frying
¼ pound (about 8 cups) arugula
Extra-virgin olive oil
½ lemon
1 cup *Salsa Rosa* (page 34)
Wedge of Parmesan cheese
1 lemon, quartered

With a meat mallet or a rolling pin, pound the veal cutlets between sheets of plastic wrap to ⅛ inch thickness. Season the cutlets with salt and pepper and press the seasonings into the meat with your fingers.

Make the coating: Combine the bread crumbs, Parmesan, parsley, salt, and pepper in a small bowl. Work in the olive oil by hand, then spread the mixture on a dinner plate. Spread the flour on another dinner plate. Break the eggs into a shallow bowl and beat lightly. Dip the cutlets in the flour, coating both sides and shaking off the excess. Then dip in the egg, letting any excess drip back into the bowl. Finally, coat the cutlets on both sides with the seasoned bread crumbs, pressing them into place. As each cutlet is coated, place it on a tray. Cover the cutlets and refrigerate until you are ready to fry them.

Heat a large skillet over high heat until very hot. Add olive oil to a depth of ¼ inch. When the oil is almost smoking, add as many cutlets as the skillet will hold comfortably; do not crowd the pan. Cook until the cutlets are golden on the bottom, about 2 minutes. Turn and cook on the second side about 30 seconds longer. With tongs, lift the cutlets as they are done, allowing any excess oil to drain back into the skillet, and transfer to several thicknesses of paper towels. Repeat with the remaining cutlets.

Place the arugula in a large bowl. Drizzle with enough extra-virgin olive oil to coat the leaves lightly. Season to taste with lemon juice, using the half lemon, and some salt and pepper. Toss, taste, and adjust the seasoning.

Divide the cutlets among 4 plates, placing them in the center. Spoon a little *Salsa Rosa* on each side of the cutlets. Mound the arugula salad on top. With a vegetable peeler, shave a little Parmesan on top of the salad. Put a lemon quarter on each plate and serve immediately.

SERVES 4

Michael's Notes: Try the same method on pounded turkey or chicken breasts or on very thin swordfish steaks.

SPIRAL-CUT FILLET OF BEEF WITH PESTO—If you have ever seen a Japanese sushi chef reduce a chunk of cucumber to a long, thin ribbon with a paring knife, you have seen a spiral cut. It's almost impossible to describe the technique in words, although you would grasp it easily if you could see it. Meats that have been spiral cut (also known as a jelly-roll cut), stuffed, rolled, and sliced like a jelly roll are popular in butcher cases, so every professional butcher knows how to do this. Ask your butcher to prepare the meat for you.

2 pounds center-cut beef fillet
   (net weight after chain and silverskin are removed)
Sea salt, preferably gray salt, and freshly ground black pepper
Basil Pesto (page 108) made with only half the oil
Extra-virgin olive oil

Ask the butcher to spiral cut or jelly-roll cut the fillet for you to create a flat, rectangular sheet of beef.

Pound the meat with the heel of your hand to a thickness of about ½ inch. Season with salt and pepper. Spread the pesto evenly over the meat, leaving a 1-inch border along one of the long sides. Starting from the opposite long side, roll the meat into a log like a jelly roll.

Using kitchen string and starting ½ inch from one end, tie the meat in 8 places at equal intervals of approximately 1 inch. Slice between the ties to create 8 pinwheels.

Prepare a hot fire in a charcoal grill, preheat a gas grill, or preheat a stove-top cast-iron grill pan over high heat. Drizzle the meat with olive oil, then grill on both sides, turning once, until done to your taste. Let rest for a few minutes, then remove the strings and serve.

SERVES 4

Michael's Notes: A fillet of beef is an expensive cut, so this is a special-occasion dish. Go to the best butcher you know, show him or her the pictures of the dish in this book, and emphasize that you need 2 pounds *after* the meat has been trimmed of its chain and silverskin.

on a roll

Once you have mastered the beef with pesto, try it with mushroom duxelles or olive tapenade.

fork tender

You'll know the meat is done when you can pull it apart with a fork.

LEFT: GRILLED PORK CHOPS WITH PECK SEASONING AND CHARRED PEPPERS, PAGE 160

CENTER: FOREVER ROASTED PORK WITH TOASTED SPICE RUB, PAGE 161

RIGHT: BABY BACK RIBS WITH ESPRESSO BBQ SAUCE, PAGE 162

GRILLED PORK CHOPS WITH PECK SEASONING **AND CHARRED PEPPERS**—I have a beloved, ridged cast-iron grill pan that I use for these pork chops and peppers, but any large griddle or a pair of cast-iron skillets will do. I like the ridged pan because it makes appetizing grill marks on the meat and keeps the chops above any dripping fat. After an initial searing, the thick chops complete their cooking in the oven while you soften the peppers in the pan.

If you've been looking for the right time to open a bottle of California Pinot Noir, it's now.

4 double-cut pork loin chops, about ¾ pound each

2 tablespoons olive oil

3 tablespoons Peck Seasoning (page 25)

4 bell peppers in assorted colors, cored, seeded and
    cut lengthwise into 1-inch-wide strips

Sea salt, preferably gray salt, and freshly ground black pepper

½ lemon, plus 4 lemon wedges for serving

Preheat the oven to 350°F. Line a roasting pan with aluminum foil, and put a flat rack in the roasting pan large enough to hold the chops.

Brush the chops with 1 tablespoon of the oil, then season all over with the Peck Seasoning, patting it into place.

Toss the bell pepper strips with the remaining 1 tablespoon oil and salt and pepper to taste.

Heat a large ridged grill pan, a griddle, or 2 cast-iron skillets over moderately high heat. Add the chops and reduce the heat to moderate. Brown the chops on both sides, about 4 minutes per side, adjusting the heat so they cook without burning the coating.

Transfer them to the prepared roasting pan. Bake until the internal temperature reaches 140°F, 25 to 30 minutes.

While the pork chops cook, reheat the pan(s) or griddle used for searing the pork. Cook the bell peppers in a single layer over moderate heat, turning them occasionally, until they are charred in spots and softened but not mushy, 8 to 10 minutes.

Transfer the pork and peppers to a warmed serving platter. Squeeze the lemon half over both and serve with the lemon wedges on the side.

SERVES 4

PICTURED ON PAGE 158

Michael's Notes: To get some nice caramelization on the bell peppers, be sure not to crowd them. If stacked, they will steam instead of sizzle.

FOREVER-ROASTED PORK WITH TOASTED SPICE RUB—I published a version of this recipe in *The Tra Vigne Cookbook*, but it is so popular that I decided to bring it back with a twist. If you loved the recipe before, now you'll have to try this variation to compare.

I got the idea for forever-roasted pork when I lived in Miami and would go to Little Havana for *lechón*, Cuban roasted pork. I've added my own seasonings, but the idea is the same: a pork shoulder cooked very slowly for a long time until it all but falls apart. Don't rush it; the anticipation is part of the pleasure. However, you can make the pork ahead and reheat it for guests. I actually prefer it at room temperature.

2 tablespoons extra-virgin olive oil, plus more for rubbing on the pork

3 cloves garlic, peeled but left whole

24 fresh sage leaves

1½ pounds onions, thinly sliced onion-soup style
   (see Michael's Notes, page 78), plus 1 onion, halved and unsliced

1 tablespoon sea salt, preferably gray salt

½ cup water

1 whole boneless pork shoulder (butt), about 6 pounds

4 tablespoons Toasted Spice Rub (page 24)

4 outer celery ribs, in 6-inch lengths

3 large carrots, peeled

Heat the 2 tablespoons olive oil in a large skillet over moderate heat. Add the garlic and cook until the cloves start to color. Add the sage and let the leaves sizzle for 10 seconds, then add the thinly sliced onions and salt and cook for 2 minutes. Add the water, cover, reduce the heat to low, and cook until the onions are quite soft, about 15 minutes. Uncover and cook until most of the liquid evaporates. Do not allow the onions to color. Let cool to room temperature.

With a boning knife, carefully cut between the muscles to open up the shoulder so that it lies flat like a book. (You can also ask the butcher to do this for you.) Rub the surface with 1 tablespoon of the spice rub, then spread the cooled onions on top.

Reshape the shoulder to enclose the onions, as if you were closing the book. Tie the pork lightly with kitchen string, taking care not to squeeze the onions out. Rub it all over with olive oil, then

with the remaining 3 tablespoons spice rub. (You can refrigerate the pork overnight at this point, but bring it to room temperature before continuing.)

Preheat the oven to 275°F. Line a roasting pan or heavy rimmed baking sheet with heavy-duty aluminum foil. Put the celery, carrots, and onion halves in the roasting pan to make a vegetable rack and top with the pork.

Roast the pork until it is fork-tender, about 7 hours. Let cool for at least 15 minutes before removing the string. Discard the vegetables; transfer the pork to a platter. To serve, pull the roast apart into large chunks with a meat fork rather than carving it into neat slices.

SERVES 8 TO 10

PICTURED ON PAGE 158

Michael's Notes: Don't try to cut the pork with a knife; just pull it apart into large chunks with a fork. Yes, it's that tender. Leftovers make fantastic tacos and sandwiches.

BABY BACK RIBS WITH ESPRESSO BBQ SAUCE — These ribs are great party food because they are easy to make in quantity and you can do the preliminary cooking hours ahead. Then, when the party gets under way, you can baste the ribs with sauce and grill them in front of your guests. They are unbelievably succulent. Serve them with Radicchio Slaw with Warm Honey Dressing (page 81) and put out lots of napkins.

3 racks baby back ribs, about 6 pounds total
Sea salt, preferably gray salt, and freshly ground black pepper

BARBECUE SAUCE:
2 tablespoons extra-virgin olive oil
2 tablespoons minced garlic
1 cup ketchup
1 cup honey
$\frac{1}{2}$ cup balsamic vinegar
$\frac{1}{4}$ cup soy sauce
$\frac{1}{4}$ cup brewed espresso

Preheat the oven to 325°F.

Cut each rack of ribs in half crosswise (between 2 ribs). Season with salt and pepper. Cover a baking sheet with heavy-duty aluminum foil. Set 3 of the half-racks side by side on the prepared baking sheet and top each with another slab.

Bake the ribs, rotating the slabs top to bottom every 30 minutes, until tender, about 2 $\frac{1}{2}$ hours. Remove the ribs from the oven and cover with a foil tent to keep them moist until you are ready to grill them.

Prepare the barbecue sauce: Heat the olive oil in a saucepan over moderately low heat. Add the garlic and sauté until it is golden. Remove from the heat and let the garlic cool in the oil. Whisk in the ketchup, honey, vinegar, soy sauce, and espresso. Simmer gently for 15 minutes to blend the flavors. Remove from the heat.

Prepare a fire in a charcoal grill, preheat a gas grill, or preheat an oven to 425°F. Brush the ribs generously with barbecue sauce. If you are grilling the ribs over charcoal, arrange the hot coals in a ring around the perimeter of the grill so that the ribs can cook in the center over indirect heat; if cooked directly over the coals, they would burn. If you are using a gas grill, adjust the flame so the ribs cook over indirect heat. Grill the ribs in a covered grill with the vents open, or bake them uncovered in the oven. Baste occasionally with additional sauce until the ribs are lightly caramelized. Transfer the rib racks to a cutting board and cut into individual riblets. Serve immediately.

SERVES 6 GENEROUSLY

PICTURED ON PAGE 159

TURKEY *POLPETTONE* WITH RADICCHIO SALAD — These highly seasoned turkey burgers have a surprise inside: an oozing nugget of mozzarella. In Italy, *polpettone* are large meatballs, and you could certainly shape these into balls and simmer them in Marinara Sauce (page 33). Instead, I make them in a burger shape and serve them with radicchio in one of my favorite boiled dressings. While you're at it, triple the dressing so you'll have some for the fridge. It will keep for several days.

SALAD:

1 small head radicchio, quartered through the core, cored, and sliced crosswise into thin ribbons

1 bunch watercress, thick stems removed

3 tablespoons fresh lemon juice

3 tablespoons honey

$\frac{1}{4}$ teaspoon sea salt, preferably gray salt

Freshly ground black pepper

$\frac{1}{4}$ cup extra-virgin olive oil

POLPETTONE:

1 pound ground turkey

$\frac{1}{2}$ cup soft fresh bread crumbs

2 tablespoons thinly sliced green onion

1 cold egg yolk

2 teaspoons chopped fresh sage

$1\frac{1}{2}$ teaspoons finely grated lemon zest

$\frac{1}{2}$ teaspoon Worcestershire sauce

1 teaspoon sea salt, preferably gray salt

Freshly ground black pepper

2 ounces whole-milk mozzarella cheese, cut into 4 equal pieces

COATING:

$\frac{1}{2}$ cup Wondra flour seasoned with salt and black pepper

1 cup soft fresh bread crumbs

1 egg

Olive oil

1 Granny Smith apple, halved and cored but not peeled

Preheat the oven to 350°F.

Make the salad: Soak, drain, and dry the radicchio according to the directions in Radicchio Slaw with Warm Honey Dressing (page 81). In a large bowl, combine the radicchio and watercress. Combine the lemon juice, honey, salt, and pepper to taste in a small skillet. Cook over moderate heat, whisking until the honey dissolves. Remove from the heat and whisk in the olive oil. Taste and adjust the seasoning. Let cool to room temperature.

Make the *polpettone*: Put the turkey in a bowl. Add remaining ingredients except for the mozzarella and work them in gently by hand. Divide the turkey into 8 equal pieces. Flatten each piece into a round patty. Top 4 of the patties with mozzarella and then with a second patty. Press the edges together.

Make the coating: Put the seasoned flour and the bread crumbs on separate sheets of waxed paper. Crack the egg into a shallow bowl and beat lightly.

Coat the patties lightly with the flour, then dip in the beaten egg, and finally in the bread crumbs, pressing the crumbs gently into place.

Heat a large ovenproof skillet over moderate heat. Add olive oil to a depth of $\frac{1}{8}$ inch. When the oil is hot, add the 4 patties. Cook on one side until nicely browned, about $1\frac{1}{2}$ minutes, then turn and cook on the second side until browned, 1 to 2 minutes longer. Transfer to the oven and cook until done throughout, about 10 minutes.

While the *polpettone* bake, slice the apple crosswise into paper-thin slices. Add to the radicchio and watercress. Toss with enough dressing to moisten, which should leave you some dressing for garnish.

To serve, divide the salad among 4 plates. Put 1 "meatball" on each plate, leaning it against the mound of salad. Drizzle the remaining dressing over the *polpettone*. Serve immediately.

SERVES 4

Michael's Notes: For the lightest *polpettone*, work the mixture as little as possible.

CHICKEN WITH ROSEMARY AND LEMON SALT—

I prefer to roast this chicken in a convection oven for a crispier skin, but if you have only a conventional oven, you'll still have a great result.

The recipe makes extra seasoned salt, which you can use on pork chops, leg of lamb, or roasted potatoes. It will keep in the refrigerator for several days or in the freezer for a month. If you prefer not to have leftover seasoning, cut the salt recipe in half.

1 chicken, about 4 pounds

SEASONED SALT:
2 tablespoons very finely minced lemon zest
2 tablespoons minced fresh rosemary
2 tablespoons sea salt, preferably gray salt
Freshly ground black pepper

3 tablespoons extra-virgin olive oil
1 or 2 fresh rosemary sprigs
1½ lemons, cut into chunks

Preheat the oven to 450°F if you have no convection fan, or to 425°F if you have a convection fan.

Rinse the chicken inside and out and dry well.

Make the salt: In a bowl, combine the lemon zest, rosemary, salt, and pepper, mixing well. Rub the chicken all over with the olive oil, then rub with 3 tablespoons of the seasoned salt. (Reserve the remaining salt for another use.) Tuck the rosemary sprigs and lemon chunks into the chicken cavity. You don't need to truss the chicken.

Place the bird on a rack in a roasting pan and roast for 15 minutes. Reduce the oven temperature by 75 degrees and continue roasting until the juices run clear when a thigh is pierced with a skewer, 50 to 55 minutes longer. Transfer the chicken to a platter and let rest for at least 15 minutes before carving.

SERVES 4

Michael's Notes: Use a vegetable peeler to remove the zest (yellow part only) from the lemons, then mince very finely. This method gives you a drier result than a grater does.

CHICKEN CACCIATORE PRONTO — Dried porcini, chopped parsley, and plenty of garlic create flavor fast in this familiar Italian "hunter's style" dish. I make my cacciatore with thighs because they're moister and better for braising than chicken breasts, and I like to serve the dish with buttered egg noodles to soak up the sauce. Note that the parsley isn't a garnish, sprinkled on top at the end just for color. It's an essential flavor that infuses the sauce, as it does so often in Italian cooking. I never take parsley for granted.

½ ounce dried porcini

1 cup warm water

8 bone-in chicken thighs, skin on

Sea salt, preferably gray salt, and freshly ground black pepper

Olive oil

1 tablespoon minced garlic

3 tablespoons finely minced fresh Italian (flat-leaf) parsley

¾ cup tomato puree (see Tomatoes, page 19)

1 cup Chicken Stock (page 22), or ½ cup canned low-sodium chicken broth mixed with ½ cup water

In a small bowl, rehydrate the porcini in the warm water for 30 minutes. Lift the porcini out with a slotted spoon and chop finely. Strain the liquid through a double thickness of damp paper towels to catch any grit. Reserve the porcini and liquid separately.

Season the chicken with salt and pepper. Heat a large skillet over high heat. Coat with a thin film of olive oil, then add the chicken, skin-side down. Brown well on the skin side, 8 to 10 minutes, reducing the heat if necessary to keep the chicken from burning. Turn and cook for about 2 minutes on the second side. Transfer the chicken to a platter and pour off all but 1 tablespoon of the fat in the skillet.

Return the skillet to moderate heat and add the garlic. Cook, stirring, until it starts to color, then add 2 tablespoons of the parsley and sauté briefly to release its fragrance. Add the porcini and stir briefly, then add the tomato puree, stock or diluted broth, and reserved porcini liquid. Bring to a simmer, return the chicken, skin-side up, to the skillet, cover, and reduce the heat to low. Cook until the chicken is no longer pink at the bone, 20 to 25 minutes.

Transfer the chicken to a warmed serving platter. Raise the heat to high and boil the sauce until it thickens, then spoon the sauce over the chicken. Top with the remaining 1 tablespoon parsley and serve at once.

SERVES 4

CHICKEN BREASTS *ALLA VENDEMMIA* — In the Napa Valley, the autumn grape harvest—*la vendemmia*, in Italian—is a season all its own. The whole valley smells like grape juice, as huge gondolas haul just-picked grapes up and down the main roads to their final winery destination. At that time of year, I might make this dish with ripe wine grapes, which are incredibly sweet. I might even sacrifice a couple of pounds from my own vineyard. (Because of the seeds, wine grapes would need to be crushed in a food mill, not a blender.)

The chicken has a lovely sauce, so I would serve it with noodles, rice, or bread to soak up every drop.

2 pounds seedless red grapes

4 large bone-in chicken breasts, skin on

Sea salt, preferably gray salt, and freshly ground black pepper

2 teaspoons Fennel Spice (page 23)

2 tablespoons extra-virgin olive oil

½ cup thinly sliced shallot

2 teaspoons minced fresh rosemary

½ cup Chicken Stock (page 22) or canned low-sodium chicken broth

---

Puree the grapes in a blender, then strain through a sieve, pressing on the solids to extract as much juice as possible. You should have about 2½ cups of juice.

Preheat the oven to 400°F. Season the chicken on all sides with salt, pepper, and Fennel Spice.

Heat a large ovenproof skillet over moderately high heat. When the skillet is hot, add the olive oil. Add the chicken breasts, skin-side down, and brown well on all sides, about 7 minutes total. Transfer the skillet to the oven and cook until the chicken is done throughout (test with a knife), 12 to 15 minutes.

Transfer the chicken to a serving platter and pour off all but 1 tablespoon of the fat in the skillet. Add the shallot to the skillet and return to moderate heat. Cook until softened, then add the rosemary and cook briefly to release its fragrance. Add 2 cups of the grape juice and simmer briskly until reduced by half. Add the stock and any collected juices from the chicken platter and simmer until the mixture has reduced to a creamy, saucelike consistency. The total volume of the sauce will be a little more than 1 cup.

Cut the chicken breasts in half with a heavy knife or cleaver and return them to the platter. Spoon the sauce over and around them. Serve immediately.

SERVES 4

Michael's Notes: I use bone-in breasts for this dish because meat always tastes better when it's cooked on the bone. If you have any leftover grape juice, pour it over ice as a treat for the chef.

LONG-COOKED HEN IN TOMATO SAUCE— Both my mother and my Aunt Mary always cooked for large groups, and they knew how to maximize their cooking equipment. Braising a hen slowly in the oven not only worked wonders on the bird, but also freed the stove top for other dishes.

Visitors to our house knew they were special if my mother prepared one of our homegrown hens. The hens were tough and sinewy, but they had excellent flavor, and the slow cooking in tomato sauce tenderized them. It also created the most spectacular pasta sauce you can imagine. We would have the chicken-flavored tomato sauce on pasta, with the chicken on the side.

⅓ cup extra-virgin olive oil

2 cups chopped onion

1 cup diced carrot

1 cup diced celery

2 tablespoons minced garlic

2 bay leaves

Sea salt, preferably gray salt

2 cups red wine

6 cans (28 ounces each) whole tomatoes, partially pureed through a meat grinder or food mill or pulsed in a blender

Freshly ground black pepper

1 chicken, about 4 pounds

½ cup minced fresh basil

¼ cup minced fresh Italian (flat-leaf) parsley

Preheat the oven to 325°F.

Heat the olive oil in a large stockpot over high heat. Add the onion, carrot, celery, garlic, bay leaves, and 1 teaspoon salt. Cook, stirring occasionally, for about 3 minutes, then reduce the heat to moderate and cook until the vegetables are lightly browned, about 20 minutes more.

Add the wine and scrape the pan bottom with a wooden spoon to loosen any flavorful stuck-on bits. Add the tomatoes, 1 tablespoon salt, and pepper to taste. Taste and add more salt if needed. It is important to add enough salt, so that the chicken seasons as it cooks.

Place the chicken, breast-side down, in the sauce, and bring to a simmer. Transfer the pot to the oven. Cook, uncovered, until the chicken is very tender, about 2 hours, spooning the sauce over the chicken from time to time. Stir in the basil and parsley and cook for 15 minutes longer. Remove from the oven and let the chicken cool in the sauce.

Serve the chicken warm with a little sauce spooned over it, or reheat the sauce separately and serve it over pasta as a first course with the chicken as a main course. Any remaining sauce can be frozen.

SERVES 4, WITH LOTS OF LEFTOVER SAUCE

Michael's Notes: If you have access to a stewing hen, by all means use it. Your sauce will be the better for it, but this dish is still quite tasty made with a young supermarket bird.

plump and juicy

Don't let the quail touch or the bacon won't crisp properly.

QUAIL WITH BACON AND HONEY—I'll never understand why Cornish game hens are so popular. Quail are much more flavorful. Fortunately, they're now more widely available, too, and the semiboneless ones make easy eating. I wrap them in bacon to add smokiness and a richness that they lack on their own, and I brush them with honey and vinegar to create an *agrodolce* (sweet-and-sour) glaze. Don't serve any forks with this dish. It's finger food.

⅓ cup honey

1 tablespoon balsamic vinegar

1 teaspoon finely chopped fresh sage

Sea salt, preferably gray salt, and freshly ground black pepper

8 semiboneless quail with wings and legs attached

8 thin slices bacon

2 tablespoons extra-virgin olive oil

½ cup dry white wine

2 fresh rosemary sprigs, each 6 inches long

1 tablespoon unsalted butter

Preheat the oven to 350°F.

In a small bowl, whisk together the honey, vinegar, sage, and salt and pepper to taste.

Season the quail with salt and pepper, then tuck the wing tips under the body of each quail. Wrap each bird with a slice of bacon. Put 2 quail side by side. Run 2 parallel skewers through both birds. Repeat with the remaining quail. Trim the skewers to fit in a skillet. Generously brush the birds with the honey mixture.

Heat the olive oil over moderately high heat in an ovenproof skillet large enough to hold all the quail. Add the quail, breast-side down, and sauté for 2 minutes. Turn and cook for 2 minutes on the back side. Transfer the skillet to the oven and bake until the quail are firm and nicely caramelized, about 15 minutes.

Transfer the quail to a serving platter and pour off any fat in the skillet. Add the wine and rosemary to the skillet and return to moderately high heat. Simmer, scraping the bottom of the skillet with a wooden spoon, until all the caramelized bits dissolve and the mixture has the consistency of a sauce. Remove from the heat and whisk in the butter. Strain the sauce through a sieve held over the quail and serve immediately.

SERVES 4

vegetables

When I'm hungry, the food I crave most isn't meat, seafood, or sweets. It's vegetables. Whatever is in season at the moment is foremost in my mind, and I am focused on how to celebrate that vegetable. In summer, I could make a meal of Skillet-Fried Corn and Tomatoes (page 179); in fall, Fennel-Roasted Vegetables (page 180); in spring, Peas and Cipolline (page 176). To me, an all-vegetable meal—with a little bread, cheese, and wine, of course—is completely satisfying.

If growers in your region have farm stands or u-pick operations, take your children or friends on an outing to buy at the source. Farmers' markets are another way to purchase directly from the producer. The closer you can get to the field in any vegetable's journey from grower to consumer, the better your produce will be. Don't forget to thank the farmers for their hard work. They often go unrecognized.

SAUTÉED GREENS WITH VINEGAR —

When I was a kid, my mom and I would pick all kinds of wild greens. It used to make my father crazy that we would pick dandelions out of other people's yards, but they weren't using them and we would. This recipe is how my mom, who was from Calabria, would prepare greens of all kinds, wild and cultivated: spinach, broccoli rabe, escarole, chard, mustard, or a mix of greens. She would make a big batch and keep it in the refrigerator, and we would eat the greens for days with crusty bread.

4 quarts spinach leaves, thick stems removed

¼ cup extra-virgin olive oil

1½ tablespoons minced garlic

Sea salt, preferably gray salt, and freshly ground black pepper

Red wine vinegar

Rinse the spinach leaves and shake in a colander to remove the excess water, but the leaves don't have to be thoroughly dry.

Heat a large pot over high heat until very hot. Add the olive oil. When the oil is almost smoking, add the garlic and cook for a few seconds until it is light brown. Add a couple of handfuls of spinach and toss with tongs, incorporating the garlic so it doesn't burn on the bottom of the pot.

Add the remaining spinach all at once, or in batches if your pot isn't large enough to hold it all at once. Toss constantly so the spinach wilts evenly. When the spinach is wilted, season with salt and pepper. Continue cooking over high heat, tossing often, until the excess liquid evaporates.

Turn the spinach out into a bowl and let it cool to room temperature, then season with wine vinegar. Eat at room temperature, or refrigerate for up to 2 days and eat cold.

SERVES 4

Michael's Notes: The wine vinegar will cause the greens to lose their beautiful green color. You can omit it, but I think it improves their taste.

ASPARAGUS WITH LEEKS AND PANCETTA —

In my house, asparagus is considered so special that we eat it three or four times a week in spring. I never tire of it, but I do find myself looking for ways to serve it other than as whole spears. When you want a break from asparagus vinaigrette, try cutting up the spears and tossing them with sautéed leeks and caramelized pancetta. Prepared that way, they're a great side dish for roast lamb, chicken, or rabbit, but you could also top them with a poached egg for lunch.

2 pounds medium asparagus

2 tablespoons extra-virgin olive oil

2 ounces thinly sliced pancetta, unrolled and cut into 1-inch lengths

1 cup thinly sliced leek, white and pale green parts only

Sea salt, preferably gray salt, and freshly ground black pepper

---

Holding an asparagus spear in both hands, bend the spear until it breaks naturally at the point where the spear becomes tough. Discard the tough end and repeat with the remaining asparagus. Cut the asparagus into 1-inch lengths.

Bring a large pot of salted water to a boil.

While the water heats, cook the olive oil and pancetta in a skillet over moderately low heat until the pancetta is almost crisp, about 5 minutes. Add the leek and sauté until softened but not colored.

Add the asparagus to the boiling water and cook until just tender, 3 to 4 minutes. Drain and add to the skillet. Season with salt and pepper and toss to coat with the seasonings.

Transfer to a serving bowl and serve immediately.

SERVES 6

PICTURED RIGHT

PEAS AND CIPOLLINE—For the first delicate spring salmon, for baby lamb chops, or for a lemony roasted chicken (page 164), I can't think of many better side dishes than this one. Fresh, sweet English peas make only a brief appearance each year. When they're available, I could eat them this way every night.

¾ pound cipolline (flat Italian onions), unpeeled

3 tablespoons unsalted butter

6 tablespoons water

Sea salt, preferably gray salt, and freshly ground black pepper

2 teaspoons minced fresh thyme

3 cups shelled English peas (about 3 pounds unshelled)

½ teaspoon minced lemon zest

Bring a large pot of water to a boil. Add the cipolline, boil for 1 minute, then drain. Peel them while they are hot; the papery outer skin should slip off easily. Trim the root end but don't remove it. Cut the onions into narrow wedges with a piece of the root attached so the wedges hold together.

Bring a pot of water to a boil for cooking the peas.

While the water heats, melt the butter in a large skillet over moderately low heat. Add the 6 tablespoons water and the onions and season with salt and pepper. Cook at a gentle bubble until the onions are tender, about 10 minutes; do not allow them to brown. Add the thyme and cook for about 1 minute to release its fragrance.

When the water boils, add the peas and cook until they are just tender, about 3 minutes. Lift them out with a skimmer or slotted spoon and add them to the skillet with the onions. Add the lemon zest and toss well. Taste and adjust the seasoning.

Transfer the vegetables to a serving bowl, then spoon a couple of tablespoons of water from the pea pot into the skillet, swirl to release any flavorful juices, and pour the juices over the peas. Serve at once.

SERVES 6

TRUE *TIELLA* — *Tiella* is the Italian name for a deep earthenware baking dish as well as for anything cooked in that dish. For me, the word conjures up a flood of memories. It reminds me of the chamomile on my aunt's breath, and of a dining table covered with a hand-crocheted cloth, small wine tumblers, and a glass decanter filled with rustic red wine. When my family returns from a successful mushroom hunt, we make this *tiella* with potatoes and porcini and a touch of tomato.

This recipe is for the *tiella* I learned from my mother. Although everyone in my extended family makes a distinctive version, they all agree on one thing: *tiella* must be made ahead for the flavors to develop and the texture to set so that it holds together when cut. Make it on a summer morning while the kitchen is still cool and have it for supper that night. The flavors only get better the next day.

Olive oil

⅓ cup extra-virgin olive oil

1 tablespoon minced garlic

1 pound spinach, thick stems removed

1 pound zucchini

1½ pounds russet potatoes, peeled

Sea salt, preferably gray salt, and freshly ground pepper

3½ cups My Mother's Tomato Sauce (page 32)

⅓ cup coarsely chopped fresh basil

½ cup freshly grated Parmesan cheese

About ⅔ cup Fine Dried Bread Crumbs (page 38)

Preheat the oven to 375°F. Lightly oil a deep 2½- to 3-quart baking dish (about 9 by 12 inches).

In a small bowl, combine the extra-virgin olive oil and garlic.

Bring a large pot of salted water to a boil and prepare a bowl of ice water. Plunge the spinach into the boiling water for about 15 seconds, then drain and transfer to the ice bath. When cool, drain again and squeeze dry. Chop coarsely and transfer to a bowl.

Trim the ends of the zucchini, then cut lengthwise into ¼-inch-thick slices. Put in a separate bowl.

Cut the potatoes in half lengthwise, put the halves cut-side down, and then cut them lengthwise into ¼-inch-thick "fingers." Put the potatoes in a third bowl.

Season the spinach, zucchini, and potatoes lightly with salt (the Parmesan will add more salt) and with pepper. Toss the vegetables with some of the garlic oil, using enough to coat them generously. Reserve any remaining oil for drizzling on top of the *tiella*.

Using half of the potatoes, make a layer in the prepared baking dish, filling in any gaps with small pieces. Spread with ½ cup of the tomato sauce, then sprinkle with 1½ tablespoons of the basil, 2 tablespoons of the Parmesan, and 2 tablespoons of the bread crumbs. Repeat the layering—vegetable, tomato sauce, basil, Parmesan, bread crumbs—using all the zucchini and then all the spinach. Top with the remaining potatoes and then the remaining tomato sauce and basil. Drizzle with the remaining garlic oil.

Cover and bake until tender and bubbling, about 1¼ hours. Uncover, sprinkle with the remaining 2 tablespoons Parmesan and the remaining 4 tablespoons bread crumbs, and continue to cook until the top browns, about 15 minutes longer. Remove from the oven and let cool to room temperature to allow the dish to settle and deepen in flavor.

Tiella may be served hot, warm, or at room temperature. Reheat in a low oven if desired. To serve, cut into squares and carefully lift out of the pan with a spatula.

SERVES 6 AS A MAIN COURSE, OR 8 TO 10 AS A SIDE DISH

Michael's Notes: In season, I replace My Mother's Tomato Sauce with fresh tomatoes that have been peeled, seeded, and chopped. I add a little more olive oil and garlic to the dish to compensate for the moisture and flavor in the sauce.

SKILLET-FRIED CORN AND TOMATOES—When you've had your fill of summer corn on the cob, try it off the cob in this quick sauté. I love the contrast of sweet corn and tart tomato, and the creaminess that comes from swirling in butter at the end. You could spoon this over grilled chicken or a burger, or serve it underneath a crisp soft-shelled crab or *spiedini* (skewers) of scallops or shrimp.

2 tablespoons olive oil

1 tablespoon minced garlic

½ teaspoon minced Calabrian chilies (see Resources, page 210)

4 cups corn kernels, from about 5 ears corn

1½ cups fresh tomato puree (see Tomatoes, page 19)

2 tablespoons unsalted butter

¼ cup thinly sliced fresh chives

Sea salt, preferably gray salt, and freshly ground black pepper

Heat a large skillet over high heat. Add the olive oil, then the garlic. Sauté until the garlic is lightly browned. Add the chilies and sauté briefly to release their character. Add the corn and cook briskly, stirring often, until partially cooked, about 3 minutes. Add the tomato puree and simmer, stirring, until the corn is just tender, about 2 minutes.

Remove from the heat, whisk in the butter, and stir in the chives. Season with salt and pepper. Transfer to a serving bowl and serve immediately.

SERVES 4

WHOLE BAKED TOMATOES—I encourage you to make a double batch of these garlicky slow-cooked tomatoes, because they're as good left over as they are the first time around. On day one, I'll serve them with a charcoal-grilled steak, lamb chops, or tuna. The next day, I chop them up and add them to hot pasta for a one-minute sauce, or spoon them over *bruschetta*. You could also add them to steamed clams, or serve them at room temperature with some feta cheese, Kalamata olives, and crusty bread.

3 pounds plum (Roma) tomatoes, peeled

¼ cup thickly sliced garlic

2 tablespoons fresh thyme leaves

Sea salt, preferably gray salt, and freshly ground black pepper

½ cup extra-virgin olive oil

Preheat the oven to 350°F. Arrange the whole tomatoes in a baking dish just large enough to hold them snugly in a single layer. Scatter the garlic and thyme leaves over them, then season generously with salt and pepper. Pour the oil over and around the tomatoes.

Bake for 1 hour, then turn the tomatoes over so they cook evenly. Lower the oven temperature to 325°F if the garlic is browning. Continue baking until the tomatoes are very tender but not collapsed, about 1 hour longer.

Remove from the oven, baste with the seasoned oil, and set aside until warm. Serve warm, not hot.

SERVES 6

FENNEL-ROASTED VEGETABLES — I think this may be one of my all-time favorite vegetable dishes. The vegetables are roasted in a hot oven with Fennel Spice until they caramelize, which gives them a depth of flavor that makes them seem almost meaty. Use this recipe as a template, substituting other vegetables as the market provides. Some, like Brussels sprouts, will need to be blanched first. More tender produce, like mushrooms or peeled winter squash, can be added without precooking. Apple wedges are a nice addition in the fall.

¾ pound Yukon Gold potatoes, unpeeled, cut into 1-inch cubes

2 large carrots, peeled and cut on the diagonal into ½-inch-thick slices

5 tablespoons extra-virgin olive oil

½ pound red onions, each halved and cut into 6 or 8 wedges through the root end

1 fennel bulb, halved lengthwise and cut into ½-inch-wide wedges through the core

¾ pound asparagus, tough ends trimmed, cut on the diagonal into 1½-inch lengths

2 zucchini, ends trimmed, halved lengthwise, and cut on the diagonal into ½-inch-thick slices

1½ tablespoons Fennel Spice (page 23), or 1 tablespoon fennel seed, crushed in a mortar or spice grinder

Sea salt, preferably gray salt

Preheat the oven to 425°F.

Put the potatoes in a large pot of cold, well-salted water. Bring to a boil, adjust the heat to maintain a gentle simmer, and cook until the potatoes are almost tender, about 7 minutes. Add the carrots and simmer for about 1 minute longer. Drain.

Heat a very large ovenproof skillet over high heat. Add 4 tablespoons of the olive oil. When the oil is hot, add the potatoes and carrots. Cook for about 1 minute, then add the onions and cook, turning occasionally with tongs, until the vegetables are nicely browned, about 10 minutes. Reduce the heat if needed to keep them from burning.

Add the fennel bulb, asparagus, zucchini, Fennel Spice or crushed fennel seed, and salt to taste. Toss well to distribute the seasonings. Drizzle with the remaining 1 tablespoon oil and toss again. Transfer the skillet to the oven and roast until the vegetables are deeply caramelized, 20 to 25 minutes, stirring them occasionally so they cook evenly. Serve immediately.

SERVES 8

PICTURED ON PAGE 182

CAULIFLOWER *ALLA PARMIGIANA* — Cauliflower is much more respected in Italy than it is in America, where its main role seems to be as an inexpensive filler on crudité platters. Italians prefer to cook it with butter and Parmesan until it's richly browned and caramelized from its natural sweetness. This is the *alla parmigiana* method, and cauliflower is only one of many vegetables prepared this way. You can use the same technique on asparagus, broccoli, fennel, zucchini, Swiss chard stems, or artichokes.

Unsalted butter for the baking dish, plus 2 ½ tablespoons
1 cauliflower, about 1 ½ pounds, separated into large florets
Sea salt, preferably gray salt, and freshly ground black pepper
⅓ cup freshly grated Parmesan cheese

Preheat the oven to 425°F. Butter an 8-by-10-inch oval baking dish, or a baking dish of equivalent size.

Bring a large pot of generously salted water to a boil. Add the florets and boil until they are slightly softened but still retain some crispness, about 4 minutes. Drain well, then slice them lengthwise so the stems are about ¼ inch thick.

Arrange the slices, overlapping them tightly, in the prepared baking dish. Season with salt and black pepper, then dot with thin slices of butter, using the 2 ½ tablespoons. Sprinkle with the Parmesan.

Bake uncovered until lightly browned on top, about 30 minutes. Serve hot.

SERVES 4

POTATOES *ALLA CONTADINA* — This potato-tomato gratin reminds me of the big roasting pans filled with potatoes that family cooks in the Italian countryside make to go with the Sunday roast or capon. That's why I call the recipe *alla contadina*, in the style of the farmhouse cook.

4 cups Cheater's Chicken Stock (page 22)
1 teaspoon sea salt, preferably gray salt
1 ½ pounds Yukon Gold potatoes, peeled and sliced lengthwise ¼-inch thick
Boiling water, if needed
Olive oil
12 Oven-Dried Tomatoes (page 37)
2 tablespoons extra-virgin olive oil or oil from the dried tomatoes
Freshly ground black pepper

Preheat the oven to 350°F.

Bring the stock and salt to a simmer in a medium saucepan, then add the potatoes. They should be barely covered with stock; if not, add boiling water. Simmer gently, uncovered, until about three-quarters done, about 8 minutes. Drain, reserving the stock. Let the potatoes cool enough to handle.

Oil an 8-by-10-inch oval baking dish, or a baking dish of equivalent size. Working from the outside toward the center, arrange the potatoes in a ring of overlapping slices, inserting a tomato half after every 4 slices. Fill in the center of the ring with more potatoes and tomatoes. You may not need all the potatoes. Moisten with 1 cup of the reserved stock, drizzle with the olive oil, and season with pepper.

Bake until the potatoes absorb most of the liquid and begin to color on top, about 1 hour, rotating the dish halfway through. Let rest for a few minutes before serving.

SERVES 4 TO 6

PICTURED ON PAGE 183

LEFT: FENNEL-ROASTED VEGETABLES, PAGE 180; RIGHT: POTATOES *ALLA CONTADINA*, PAGE 181

POTATOES "DA DELFINA" — Outside of Florence is a famous restaurant called Da Delfina, which is renowned for serving locally foraged herbs and wild game. That's where I first had potatoes prepared this way, boiled with good salt, cooled slightly, and smashed between the cook's palms to break the skin. Finally, the "smashed" potatoes are browned in olive oil until they are crusty outside and creamy within. Serve as a side dish with a simple roasted meat, and they will steal the show.

1½ pounds (about 16) small "creamer" potatoes, preferably Yukon Gold
Peanut oil
Sea salt, preferably gray salt, and freshly ground black pepper
¼ cup chopped fresh Italian (flat-leaf) parsley

2 teaspoons grated lemon zest
¼ cup extra-virgin olive oil
¼ cup chopped garlic

Put the potatoes in a large pot of cold, well-salted water to cover. Bring to a boil and cook until a knife slips in easily, 15 to 20 minutes. Drain the potatoes. When they are cool enough to handle, hold one between your hands as if you were clapping and press gently with the heel of one hand. You want to smash the potato to about a ½-inch thickness while keeping it in one piece. The skin will split, but the potato should not fall apart. Repeat with the remaining potatoes. You can prepare the potatoes to this point several hours ahead.

Pour ½ inch of peanut oil in a large skillet and heat over moderately high heat.

When the oil begins to smoke, carefully put the smashed potatoes in the oil and cook on both sides until crisp and well browned, 8 to 10 minutes. With a slotted spoon, transfer to paper towels to drain. Season with salt and pepper.

While the potatoes cook, combine the parsley and lemon zest in a serving bowl. Heat the olive oil in a small skillet over moderately high heat. Add the garlic and sauté until lightly browned. With a slotted spoon, transfer the garlic to the bowl with the parsley-lemon mixture.

When the potatoes are ready, add them to the garlic mixture and toss gently. Serve immediately. Save the leftover garlic oil and use it to dress a salad or vegetables the following day.

SERVES 4

SAUTÉED MUSHROOMS—These richly browned mushrooms are the first dish I ever cooked well, while still a teenager in California's Central Valley. The key to success is being patient. You want to avoid stirring them at first so they get deeply caramelized and don't release a lot of liquid.

Although a lot of cooks look down on button mushrooms, I'm a big fan. You just have to handle them right. Don't rinse them or they'll take up water; just wipe them with a damp cloth or brush them with a mushroom brush to clean.

These garlicky mushrooms may be the dish I'm asked to make most often. They're a terrific side dish for steak, but I also serve them at room temperature as an antipasto. Once you master the technique, you'll be making them again and again, too.

6 tablespoons extra-virgin olive oil

1½ pounds fresh button mushrooms, halved if large or left whole if small

2 tablespoons unsalted butter

Sea salt, preferably gray salt, and freshly ground black pepper

1 tablespoon minced garlic

1½ teaspoons minced fresh thyme

1½ tablespoons fresh lemon juice

½ cup dry white wine

1 tablespoon chopped fresh Italian (flat-leaf) parsley

Heat a large skillet over high heat. Add the olive oil. When the oil is hot, sprinkle in the mushrooms in a single layer. Don't stir! Let them sizzle until they have caramelized on the bottom, about 2 minutes. If you toss them too soon, they will release their liquid and begin to steam. When the bottoms are caramelized, toss the mushrooms and continue to cook over high heat for about 5 minutes. Drain the mushrooms in a sieve and discard the excess oil.

Return the mushrooms to the skillet and add the butter. Continue to cook, stirring occasionally, until the mushrooms are beautifully browned, 2 to 3 minutes. Season with salt and pepper and add the garlic. Sauté until the garlic is lightly browned, about 2 minutes. Add the thyme and lemon juice and cook until the liquid evaporates. Add the wine, reduce the heat slightly, and simmer until the mushrooms are glazed with the sauce. Add the parsley, transfer to a warmed bowl, and serve immediately.

SERVES 4

Michael's Notes: If you're sautéing chicken for dinner, cook the mushrooms in the same pan after you've removed the chicken. They'll pick up a lot of meaty flavor.

be patient

To caramelize the mushrooms, don't stir too soon.

sweet things

Dessert wasn't a daily occurrence in my childhood home. In the Italian tradition, we mostly had sweets on special occasions: on holidays, for example, or when all the relatives got together. I still don't have a serious sweet tooth and would rather have any dessert a couple of hours after dinner, when I can appreciate it more.

Because I'm a more accomplished cook than a baker, my favorite desserts don't call for elaborate maneuvers. Most often, they are simple and fruit-based, like Strawberries *Pazzo* (page 190), *Pesche alla Nonna* (page 197), or Fresh Cherry *Crostata* (page 191). I do love to end a meal with cheese and will often accompany the cheese with something that complements it, like Balsamic-Glazed Fruits (page 204) or Dried Fruit Compote with Sambuca (page 202).

STRAWBERRIES *PAZZO* — This is a palate-shocking dish that I learned from a very traditional woman: Lorenza de' Medici, owner of Badia a Coltibuono, the Tuscan wine-and-oil estate. When I visited her there, we had wild strawberries picked on her property. They were dipped in old *balsamico* with sugar and cracked black pepper, and I'll never forget that surprising taste. Back in Napa Valley, I embellished the idea a bit, adding biscotti and mascarpone to make a dessert that always leaves a lasting impression on my guests.

¼ cup superfine sugar

3 tablespoons balsamic vinegar

Sea salt, preferably gray salt, and freshly ground black pepper

3 cups strawberries, hulled and quartered lengthwise

4 biscotti, each about 6 inches long

¼ pound mascarpone cheese, beaten smooth with a spoon

In a bowl, whisk together the sugar, vinegar, and a generous pinch of the salt and pepper. About 15 minutes before serving, add the berries and toss gently until they are well coated. Gently crush 1 biscotto into each of 4 serving bowls. Top with the marinated strawberries, dividing them evenly. Put a dollop of mascarpone cheese on each serving and serve immediately.

SERVES 4

PICTURED ON PAGE 193

Michael's Notes: For an alternative presentation, put a single biscotto upright in a glass. Spoon the marinated berries into the glass, then top with frozen yogurt or gelato.

WARM RICE PUDDING WITH SUMMER FRUITS — If you keep it creamy, not stiff, and serve it warm, rice pudding can be almost like a custard sauce for summer fruit.

1 quart milk

⅓ cup granulated sugar

Salt

2 lemon zest strips

½ vanilla bean, split lengthwise

½ cup water

¾ cup Arborio rice

3 egg yolks

1 teaspoon fresh lemon juice

4 cups mixed summer fruits, such as strawberries, peaches, apricots, blackberries, blueberries, or figs, in any combination, sliced as needed

Superfine sugar (optional)

Combine the milk, granulated sugar, a pinch of salt, lemon zest, vanilla bean, and water in a wide saucepan or straight-sided skillet. Bring to a simmer over moderate heat, stirring to dissolve the sugar. Add the rice and simmer gently, stirring occasionally, until the grains are tender and the milk is slightly thickened, about 20 minutes.

In a bowl, beat the yolks with the lemon juice until well blended. Whisk in about 1 cup of the hot rice to warm the egg mixture, then pour the mixture into the rice. Cook briefly, stirring constantly, until the pudding visibly thickens, about 1 minute. Remove from the heat and remove and discard the lemon zest and vanilla bean. Let the rice pudding cool until it is just warm; it will thicken as it cools.

If the fruits need a little sweetening, add superfine sugar to taste. Divide the fruits among 6 or 8 plates or balloon wineglasses. Spoon the warm rice pudding over the top. Alternatively, alternate layers of fruit and warm pudding in parfait glasses.

SERVES 6 TO 8

PICTURED ON PAGE 192

FRESH CHERRY *CROSTATA* — Fresh cherry season never lasts long enough for me. During the few weeks that I can get cherries, I try to use them in as many simple ways as I can. This rustic *crostata* is a favorite because it looks like it came out of a loving grandmother's oven. The warm, softened cherries glisten in the center, and there's just enough flaky, sugar-dusted pastry to support them. Serve it warm from the oven with vanilla or almond ice cream. You can also combine fruits: try cherries with apricots or nectarines.

I highly recommend using a pizza stone. They're not expensive, and the *crostata* bakes so much better on one. Be sure to preheat it thoroughly.

TART DOUGH:

2 ½ cups unbleached all-purpose flour

2 tablespoons granulated sugar

2 teaspoons salt

1 cup (½ pound) chilled unsalted butter, cut into tablespoon-size pieces

¼ cup ice water, or more if needed

1 teaspoon pure vanilla extract

FILLING:

4 cups pitted fresh cherries

¼ cup granulated sugar

1 tablespoon unbleached all-purpose flour

¼ teaspoon ground cinnamon

1 egg yolk beaten with 1 tablespoon heavy cream for egg wash

2 teaspoons coarse sugar (see Resources, page 210)

Make the tart dough: Combine the flour, granulated sugar, and salt in a food processor and pulse to blend. Add the butter and pulse until the mixture forms coarse crumbs. Stir together the ¼ cup ice water and the vanilla and sprinkle it over the mixture in the processor. Pulse just until a dough forms, adding a little extra ice water if necessary. Divide the dough in half, and shape each half into a 1-inch-thick round. Wrap 1 disk tightly in plastic wrap and refrigerate for at least 1 hour; freeze the other for a future use.

Put a pizza stone in the oven and preheat the oven to 425°F for 45 minutes. Remove the dough from the refrigerator about 15 minutes before rolling to soften it slightly.

Place the dough round between 2 sheets of parchment paper and roll into a 13-inch round, flouring the round lightly as needed to keep the dough from sticking. Remove the top sheet of parchment. Slide a pizza peel or rimless baking sheet under the bottom sheet of parchment.

Make the filling: Combine the cherries, granulated sugar, flour, and cinnamon in a bowl and toss well. Fill the center of the dough round with the cherries in an even layer, leaving a border of about 1½ inches. Fold the border up and over the cherries to make a rim. Brush the rim with egg wash, then sprinkle with coarse sugar. Trim the excess parchment with scissors.

Use the pizza peel or baking sheet to transfer the *crostata*, still with parchment underneath, to the oven, sliding it, along with the paper, directly onto the pizza stone. Bake until the crust is nicely browned and the cherries are bubbling, about 40 minutes. Remove from the oven with the peel or baking sheet and let cool on a rack for 15 minutes before serving. Serve warm.

SERVES 8

PICTURED ON PAGE 194

Michael's Notes: You may be tempted to pit and sugar the cherries well ahead of time, but please don't. They quickly start to discolor and throw off juice. You can pit them an hour or two before baking, but don't add sugar until the last minute.

LEFT AND RIGHT: ROSEMARY SANDCAKE, PAGE 196; CENTER: FRESH CHERRY CROSTATA, PAGE 191

ROSEMARY SANDCAKE WITH SUMMER BERRIES — This recipe is adapted from one given to me by Marta Pulini, now the chef at Coco Pazzo in New York. After I tasted Marta's splendid cake, she took me to Mantua, where I tasted the cake made by the women who taught her how to make it. Its Italian name is *torta sabbiosa* (sandy cake), due to its incredibly fine, sandlike texture. It doesn't store well, so make it the day you plan to eat it. And, yes, the recipe is correct. The batter goes into a cold oven.

CAKE:

Unsalted butter and unbleached all-purpose flour

1⅓ cups sifted potato starch (*not* potato flour)

1½ teaspoons baking powder

1 cup (½ pound) unsalted butter, at room temperature

1 cup plus 1 tablespoon superfine sugar

3 eggs, separated

2 tablespoons grated lemon zest

1 tablespoon finely minced fresh rosemary

½ teaspoon pure vanilla extract

FOR SERVING:

Confectioners' sugar

3 pints mixed summer berries or 6 peaches, peeled and sliced, or a combination

Granulated sugar

Lightly whipped heavy cream

Thoroughly butter the bottom and sides of a 9-inch round cake pan with 2-inch sides. Line the bottom with a round of parchment paper. Coat the sides of the pan with flour, shaking out the excess.

Make the cake: Sift the potato starch and baking powder into a bowl. In an electric mixer, cream the butter until smooth. Add the 1 cup superfine sugar gradually, beating until well blended. Add the egg yolks one at a time, beating well after each addition and scraping down the sides of the bowl once or twice. Beat in the lemon zest, rosemary, and vanilla. By hand, stir in the dry ingredients just until blended.

Beat the egg whites and the remaining 1 tablespoon superfine sugar to soft peaks. Fold half the beaten whites into the potato starch mixture to lighten it, then gently fold in the remaining whites. Transfer the batter to the prepared pan, leveling it with a spatula.

Place in a cold oven and turn the thermostat to 350°F. Bake until the cake is well risen, nicely browned, and beginning to pull away from the sides of the pan, 50 to 55 minutes. Let cool completely in the pan on a rack, then invert onto the rack and carefully remove the parchment paper. Invert again onto a serving platter. Put the confectioner's sugar in a sieve and dust the surface of the cake lightly with it.

About 30 minutes before serving, put the fruit in a bowl, add granulated sugar to taste, and crush the fruit with a fork until it is roughly mashed. Let it stand 30 minutes to render some juice.

Cut the cake into 12 slices. Serve a slice of cake with crushed fruit spooned over and around it and a dollop of whipped cream on the top or alongside.

SERVES 12

PICTURED ON PAGES 194 AND 195

Michael's Notes: Most supermarkets stock potato starch with the baking ingredients.

PESCHE ALLA NONNA — When I was little and dinner was over, I remember my grandmother in her hard-soled shoes going into the pantry in the garage for her canned peaches. She would put a little vanilla gelato on top and watch me as I tipped the bowl to get every last drop.

6 small, ripe but slightly firm peaches

1 cup granulated sugar

2-inch piece vanilla bean

Juice of ½ lemon

2 ½ cups water

1 pint raspberries

Superfine sugar (optional)

Vanilla ice cream

6 amaretti cookies

Peel the peaches with a vegetable peeler but leave whole.

Combine the granulated sugar, vanilla bean, lemon juice, and water in a saucepan. Bring to a simmer over moderate heat, stirring to dissolve the sugar. Add the peaches, cover, and adjust the heat to maintain a gentle simmer. Poach the peaches until they are barely tender, about 4 minutes; they will continue to cook as they cool. Remove them from the poaching liquid with a slotted spoon; reserve the syrup. When they are cool, halve the peaches and remove the pits.

Strain the syrup, let cool thoroughly, then pour it over the peach halves. Cover and refrigerate the peaches.

Put the raspberries in a blender with ½ cup of the syrup from the chilled peaches. Blend until smooth, then strain through a fine-mesh sieve to remove the seeds. Thin the raspberry sauce if needed with a little more syrup. Taste and add a little superfine sugar if the sauce needs sweetening.

To serve, cut each peach half into 3 slices. Make a pool of raspberry sauce on each of 6 dessert plates. Put a scoop of ice cream in the center. Surround with the peach slices. Crumble an amaretti cookie over the top and serve.

SERVES 6

Michael's Notes: You'll have an easier time pitting the peaches if you buy a freestone variety, but clingstone peaches will work. Don't peel the peaches ahead of time; they deteriorate quickly.

APPLE *CLAFOUTI* — *Clafouti* is a country French baked pudding, versatile enough to serve for breakfast, brunch, tea, or dinner, and suited to a wide variety of fruits. Cherries, plums, and other stone fruits work well, and I've also made savory *clafoutis* with fresh corn and mushrooms.

I think it's charming to cook and serve this from a cast-iron pan—especially mini pans that make individual servings—but you can use decorative porcelain pie dishes, individual gratin dishes, or any skillet providing it is not nonstick. *Clafouti* tastes and looks best served directly from the oven, while it's puffy and light. It can also be served at room temperature, but it will settle in the pan as it cools.

BATTER:

½ cup unbleached all-purpose flour

⅓ cup plus 2 teaspoons granulated sugar

¼ teaspoon ground cinnamon

Salt

3 eggs plus 1 egg yolk

1 cup milk

APPLES:

¼ vanilla bean, split lengthwise

2 tablespoons unsalted butter

1½ cups peeled and diced Granny Smith apple (½-inch dice; about 1 large apple)

2 tablespoons granulated sugar

1 teaspoon grappa, Calvados, or other fruit brandy

Confectioners' sugar

⅓ cup crème fraîche

Preheat the oven to 400°F.

Make the batter: Sift the flour, granulated sugar, cinnamon and a pinch of salt into a bowl. In a separate bowl, whisk the eggs, egg yolk, and milk until well blended. Add about one-third of the egg mixture to the flour mixture and whisk to form a paste, then gradually incorporate the remaining egg mixture. Whisk until well blended.

Cook the apples: With the tip of a knife, scrape the vanilla bean seeds from the pod into an ovenproof medium cast-iron or stainless-steel skillet. Add the pod and the butter and cook over moderately high heat until the butter turns nut brown. Add the apple and cook, stirring often, for about 3 minutes to soften it. Remove the vanilla bean pod and discard. Sprinkle the apple with the granulated sugar,

reduce the heat to moderately low, and cook until the apple is about three-fourths done and the sugar has melted and is coating the apple in a light syrup. Add the grappa or other brandy, swirl the skillet briefly, then spread the fruit evenly in the skillet.

Remove the skillet from the heat. Working quickly, pour the batter through a sieve evenly over the fruit. Bake until the edges of the *clafouti* are puffed and browned and the center is set, about 15 minutes. Remove from the oven.

Put some confectioners' sugar in a sieve and generously dust the surface of the *clafouti*. Serve warm directly from the skillet with a dollop of crème fraîche.

SERVES 6

Michael's Notes: If you plan to serve individual *clafoutis* from mini pans, heat the pans in the oven until quite hot, about 5 minutes, then divide the cooked fruit among the pans, top with the batter, and bake. Cooking time will vary depending on the size of the pans. To make a cherry *clafouti*, use 1¼ cups pitted cherries. Substitute 1 teaspoon grated lemon zest for the cinnamon and Grand Marnier for the grappa.

light and fluffy

Whisk the zabaglione just until it holds a soft peak.

ITALIAN FRUIT SALAD WITH *STA BENE* HONEY ZABAGLIONE — Italians often serve a macerated fruit salad *(macedonia)* for dessert, and its contents will typically change with the seasons. I've used summer fruits here, but you could follow the same outline to make a winter *macedonia* with pineapple, bananas, oranges, apples, and grapes. Change the liqueur to rum or sambuca, if you prefer.

The honey zabaglione stays stable for a couple of days, which is why I call it *sta bene*, which loosely means that it holds well. You can serve the zabaglione chilled or, if you like, you can make it in front of your guests and serve it at room temperature.

FRUIT SALAD:

½ pint strawberries, hulled and sliced

½ pound apricots, plums, or pluots, sliced

2 peaches, peeled if desired, sliced

½ pint blueberries

2 tablespoons Cointreau or other orange liqueur

1 tablespoon superfine sugar, or more to taste

1 teaspoon grated lemon zest

ZABAGLIONE:

6 egg yolks

¼ cup honey

½ cup dry white wine

¾ cup heavy cream, whipped to firm peaks

Make the fruit salad: In a large bowl, combine the strawberries, apricots, peaches, and blueberries. Add the Cointreau, 1 tablespoon sugar, and lemon zest. Toss gently, taste, and add more sugar if desired. Refrigerate for at least 2 hours or up to 8 hours.

Make the zabaglione: In a large stainless-steel bowl or the top pan of a double boiler, whisk the egg yolks with the honey until blended. Set the bowl over—not touching—simmering water and whisk vigorously until the mixture lightens in color and thickens and the whisk leaves a trail, about 3 minutes. Add the wine and continue whisking constantly until the mixture is pale, thick, and greatly expanded in volume, about 10 minutes. The mixture will curdle if it gets too hot, so whisk it off the heat for a few seconds if you fear the eggs are cooking too fast.

When the zabaglione is light, fluffy, and capable of holding a soft peak, transfer the bowl to a larger bowl filled with ice water to cool the zabaglione quickly. When cool, fold in the whipped cream. Use immediately or cover and refrigerate for up to 2 days.

To serve, divide the fruit among 6 compote dishes or small plates. Put a dollop of zabaglione alongside.

SERVES 6

DRIED FRUIT COMPOTE WITH SAMBUCA—

This quick compote is a good choice for a winter dinner when you have little time to cook but want to make an impression. You can prepare it ahead (it's better made ahead), then spoon it over store-bought ice cream to create an original and memorable dessert. I also like it with blue cheese at the end of a meal, especially if there's a dessert wine on the table.

1 cup dried peaches or nectarines, cut into ¼-inch-wide strips

1 cup dried pears, cut into ¼-inch-wide strips

1 cup dried apricots, cut into ¼-inch-wide strips or quartered

½ cup golden raisins

½ cup dried cherries

2 cups water

1 cup sugar

2 whole cloves

1-inch piece cinnamon stick

2 lemon zest strips, left whole or julienned

1 tablespoon fresh lemon juice

1 tablespoon sambuca or other anise liqueur

Put the peaches, pears, apricots, raisins, and cherries in a bowl.

Combine the water, sugar, cloves, cinnamon, and lemon zest in a saucepan. Bring slowly to a simmer, stirring to dissolve the sugar. Simmer for 1 minute, then pour the syrup over the fruit. Let stand until cool, stirring occasionally, then stir in the lemon juice and sambuca. Refrigerate until well chilled.

MAKES ABOUT 5 CUPS

mighty fine

Use a sharp knife to slice lemon zest strips into fine julienne for a more refined presentation.

BALSAMIC-GLAZED FRUITS — Apples and pears slowly dried in the oven develop an intense flavor and a texture that's not quite fruit leather but close. I add butter, brown sugar, and balsamic vinegar so that a glaze cloaks the fruits as they cook. You can serve them warm over a grilled pork chop, but I particularly like them with the cheese course, especially with blue cheeses. Use a good-quality balsamic here—maybe not your twenty-five-year-old vinegar, but a step up from supermarket brands.

5 tablespoons fresh lemon juice

4 large pears, peeled, cored, and each cut into 8 wedges

2 large apples, peeled, cored, and each cut into 8 wedges

3 tablespoons unsalted butter

1 teaspoon finely chopped fresh rosemary

2 bay leaves

$\frac{1}{3}$ cup balsamic vinegar

$\frac{1}{3}$ cup firmly packed light brown sugar

Sea salt, preferably gray salt, and freshly ground black pepper

Preheat the oven to 250°F.

Measure 2 tablespoons lemon juice into a large nonreactive bowl. Add the pears and apples to the bowl and toss to coat.

Melt the butter in a nonreactive roasting pan or rimmed baking sheet over moderate heat. Cook until it stops foaming and turns light brown. Add the rosemary, bay leaves, vinegar, brown sugar, and the remaining 3 tablespoons lemon juice. Bring to a boil, stirring to dissolve the brown sugar, then simmer until reduced almost to a glaze.

Season the fruits with a pinch of salt and pepper and add to the roasting pan. Stir well to coat the wedges evenly.

Spread the wedges in the pan in a single layer and place in the oven. Cook slowly until the fruit is soft, supple, well glazed, and concentrated in flavor, about 6 hours. Turn the wedges over every hour for at least the first 3 hours. To test whether the fruit is ready, remove a piece and let it cool for a few minutes. Taste to see if the flavor is intense enough for your palate. Do not let the fruit get as dry as a fruit leather. Remove any pieces that are done before the rest.

Remove the fruit from the oven, let cool completely, and store in a tightly sealed container. Refrigerate if you don't plan to use it within 2 days, but bring it to room temperature or warm it gently before serving. The fruit will keep a week or more in the refrigerator.

MAKES ABOUT 4 CUPS

MASCARPONE CHEESECAKE — I still remember my first taste of mascarpone—at Peck, the fancy food shop in Milan. It was nuttier, silkier, and much more seductive than stiff American sour cream. To have a slice of cheesecake made from this luscious cultured cream strikes me as a true luxury.

Unsalted butter or vegetable oil cooking spray

1½ cups fine biscotti crumbs (made in a food processor) or other cookie crumbs

2 tablespoons unsalted butter, melted

6 ounces cream cheese, at room temperature

½ cup sugar

3 eggs

2 tablespoons fresh lemon juice

1 teaspoon grated lemon zest

1 pound mascarpone cheese

Boiling water

Butter or spray the bottom and sides of a 9-inch springform pan. Wrap the outside of the pan with 2 layers of heavy-duty aluminum foil to prevent leakage. The foil should come all the way up the sides of the pan because the cheesecake will bake in a water bath.

In a bowl, mix the crumbs and butter well. Pat the mixture firmly into place on the bottom of the prepared pan and refrigerate for 1 hour.

Preheat the oven to 350°F.

In an electric mixer, beat the cream cheese until smooth. Add the sugar gradually and beat until completely blended. Add the eggs one at a time, beating well after each addition and scraping down the sides of the bowl once or twice. Add the lemon juice and lemon zest, then add the mascarpone and beat until smooth. Pour into the prepared pan.

Place the cake pan in a larger pan and add boiling water to come halfway up the sides of the cake pan. Bake for 1 hour, rotating the pan after 30 minutes for even cooking. It will be lightly colored on the top. Remove from the oven and let cool in the water bath. As it cools, it will shrink a little from the sides of the pan.

When completely cool, remove the pan sides and slide the cheesecake onto a plate. Cover and refrigerate. Serve chilled.

SERVES 10

Michael's Notes: You'll need about ½ pound biscotti to make the 1½ cups crumbs for the crust.

CARAMEL *PANNA COTTA*—*Panna cotta* is definitely one of the easiest desserts you can make, with the added advantage that it can be ready hours before your guests arrive. I had never tasted a caramel version, but I liked the idea and decided to create one. I think you'll like the result. Serve it with fresh figs, cherries, or a cherry compote in summer, or with caramelized apples or pears in winter.

Like many professional cooks, I prefer gelatin leaves to powdered gelatin. I believe they give gelled desserts like *panna cotta* a more pleasing texture.

½ cup superfine sugar
2 tablespoons water
3 cups heavy cream
2 ½ gelatin leaves (see Resources, page 210)

Combine the sugar and water in a heavy saucepan. Stir until all the sugar is moistened, then place over moderately low heat and cook without stirring. Watch carefully as the sugar liquefies and begins to darken. When the sugar has turned a rich golden brown—do not let it darken too much—add the cream all at once, being careful as it may spatter and burn you. The sugar will seize into a clump immediately, but as the cream warms, the sugar will dissolve. Keep stirring patiently with a wooden spoon, scraping up the undissolved caramel on the bottom of the pan, until all the caramel has dissolved and the mixture has turned a pale butterscotch color.

Meanwhile, soak the gelatin leaves in a large bowl of cold water until soft, 4 to 5 minutes. Squeeze gently to remove excess water, then add the gelatin to the warm sweetened cream. Stir until the gelatin melts, about 30 seconds, then strain through a sieve.

Ladle into six 4- to 5-ounce molds. Cover and refrigerate until firm, several hours or overnight. To unmold, run a knife under hot water until the knife is hot, wipe it dry, then run it around the inside edge of each mold and invert onto individual plates.

MAKES 6 SERVINGS

Michael's Notes: Don't let the caramel get too dark before adding the cream, or your *panna cotta* will taste burnt. And please be careful when you add the cream. Spattering caramel can cause a nasty burn.

MOCK MISÙ—Because I love to cook but have never cared much about baking, I'm always looking to add to my repertoire of cooks' desserts—recipes you don't have to be a precision baker to pull off. Here's a good example, a *tiramisù* variation that calls for brandy-soaked ladyfingers, sweetened ricotta, and grated chocolate. It couldn't be easier.

¾ cup sugar

¼ cup brandy or rum

½ cup water

4 cups Homemade Ricotta (page 39) or whole-milk ricotta cheese

½ teaspoon pure vanilla extract

6 tablespoons grated bittersweet chocolate

18 ladyfingers

Combine the sugar, brandy or rum, and water in a small saucepan. Bring to a boil over moderate heat, stirring to dissolve the sugar. Remove from the heat, transfer to a shallow bowl, and let cool.

In a large bowl, stir to combine the ricotta, vanilla, and ½ cup of the cooled syrup. Fold in 4 tablespoons of the grated chocolate.

Choose a dish that measures about 7 by 10 inches. One at a time, dunk half the ladyfingers in the brandy syrup to moisten them well, then arrange them in a single layer in the bottom of the dish. Spread half the ricotta mixture evenly over the ladyfingers. Moisten the remaining ladyfingers with the remaining syrup and arrange them over the ricotta. Top with the rest of the ricotta, spreading it evenly. Sprinkle the top with the remaining 2 tablespoons grated chocolate. Cover and refrigerate for several hours before serving.

SERVES 8

PICTURED ON FOLLOWING PAGE

CHOCOLATE ESPRESSO GELATO—I love the character that a hint of coffee adds to a chocolate dessert. You can lose interest in a pure chocolate cake or ice cream after a few bites, but adding coffee to chocolate creates another dimension that makes you want to keep eating. Serve this rich mocha ice cream on its own or topped with some chopped chocolate or chocolate nibs (see Resources, page 210).

1½ cups milk

1½ cups heavy cream

¾ cup sugar

1 vanilla bean

2 teaspoons ground espresso-roast coffee

6 egg yolks

½ cup (about 2¼ ounces) finely chopped bittersweet chocolate

Combine the milk, cream, sugar, vanilla bean, and espresso in a saucepan. Bring to a simmer over moderately low heat, stirring to dissolve the sugar.

Meanwhile, in a small bowl, whisk the egg yolks until blended. When the milk mixture simmers, gradually whisk about ½ cup of the hot milk mixture into the eggs to warm them, then pour the warmed eggs into the saucepan, stirring constantly. Cook over moderately low heat, stirring with a wooden spoon, until the mixture visibly thickens and reaches 175°F on an instant-read thermometer. Do not let the mixture boil or it will curdle.

Immediately remove from the heat and strain the custard through a fine sieve into a bowl. Add the chocolate, whisking until it melts. Let the mixture cool, then cover and refrigerate to chill thoroughly. Freeze in an ice cream freezer according to the manufacturer's directions.

MAKES ABOUT 1 QUART, TO SERVE 6

PICTURED ON PAGE 209

Michael's Notes: After straining the custard, you can rinse and dry the vanilla bean and reuse it in another dessert.

LEFT: MOCK MISÙ, PAGE 207; RIGHT: CHOCOLATE ESPRESSO GELATO, PAGE 207

ACKNOWLEDGMENTS

RESOURCES

Michael Chiarello's Casual Cooking is a collection of my personal comfort foods. It includes dishes that I grew up with, dishes that harbor memories, foods that were part of the fabric of my childhood. As the father of three daughters, I've tried to preserve these recipes for them and to expand the heritage with my own inventions—dishes that I hope will become their traditions.

I was fortunate to have Janet Fletcher, one of the most talented food writers around, as my co-author. She spent hours with me in the kitchen, carefully recording and testing each recipe, translating my often far-flung ideas into dishes that work for home cooks.

I had always wanted to work with superstar photographer Deborah Jones. She has a way of bringing out the best, not only in the food she photographs, but also in everyone around her. She filled our photo shoots with beautiful music, great breakfasts, *The New York Times,* and hot Peet's coffee. It was a pleasure just to watch her work.

Deborah's photo team of Sara Slavin (prop styling), Sandra Cook (food styling), Heidi Ladendorf, and Jeri Jones made us feel so at home and part of a true collaboration.

Cliff 'n' Dave—Cliff Morgan and Dave Hughes from Level, plus their assistants Stephanie Marquardt and Kim Wedlake—were our stellar design team. They never said "not possible," and they always had more killer ideas than we had pages in the book. I will never forget the thrill I felt when I saw our book tacked up in their offices. They always "got it."

David Shalleck, NapaStyle's culinary director, worked with Janet and me throughout the project, from development through photography. His talent, amazing palate and spirit always inspire me. David's assistant, Claudia Sansone, worked at our side, always with a smile on her face.

To Susie Heller, NapaStyle's vice president of media and, most of all, my "bud": Thank you for once again bringing a dream of mine to reality. You have brought so much joy to me, my team, and my family. We will never let you move back to Cleveland!

Of course, none of this would have been possible without Bill LeBlond, Vivien Sung, and Chronicle Books. Thank you for your patience through the many evolutions of this idea. This is the fourth cookbook that we've done together, and it won't be the last.

Tante grazie a tutti.

FOR BALSAMIC VINEGAR, BRITTANY GRAY SALT, CALABRIAN CHILIES, CALIFORNIA-GROWN ARBORIO RICE, CALIFORNIA OLIVE OIL, FENNEL SPICE RUB, TOASTED SPICE RUB, HERBES DE NAPA, SCHARFFEN BERGER CHOCOLATE AND CHOCOLATE NIBS:

www.napastyle.com
866-776-6272 (toll free)

FOR LEAF GELATIN AND COARSE SUGAR:

The Baker's Catalogue
P. O. Box 876
Norwich, VT 05055-0876
800-827-6836
www.bakerscatalogue.com

FOR DRIED LAVENDER FLOWERS:

Kalustyan's
123 Lexington Avenue
New York, NY 10016
212-685-3451

FOR CALIFORNIA CHILI POWDER:

Sold in many Mexican markets, California chili powder is a pure chili powder, not a blend of seasonings, and it is mild. A good substitute is ancho chili powder from www.penzeys.com.

FOR POINT REYES ORIGINAL BLUE CHEESE:

Point Reyes Farmstead Cheese Company
415-663-8880
Or print out a faxable order form from www.pointreyescheese.com.

INDEX

TABLE OF EQUIVALENTS—The exact equivalents in the following tables have been rounded for convenience.

LIQUID/DRY MEASURES

U.S.	METRIC
$\frac{1}{4}$ teaspoon	1.25 milliliters
$\frac{1}{2}$ teaspoon	2.5 milliliters
1 teaspoon	5 milliliters
1 tablespoon (3 teaspoons)	15 milliliters
1 fluid ounce (2 tablespoons)	30 milliliters
$\frac{1}{4}$ cup	60 milliliters
$\frac{1}{3}$ cup	80 milliliters
$\frac{1}{2}$ cup	120 milliliters
1 cup	240 milliliters
1 pint (2 cups)	480 milliliters
1 quart (4 cups, 32 ounces)	960 milliliters
1 gallon (4 quarts)	3.84 liters
1 ounce (by weight)	28 grams
1 pound	454 grams
2.2 pounds	1 kilogram

LENGTH

U.S.	METRIC
$\frac{1}{8}$ inch	3 millimeters
$\frac{1}{4}$ inch	6 millimeters
$\frac{1}{2}$ inch	12 millimeters
1 inch	2.5 centimeters

OVEN TEMPERATURE

FAHRENHEIT	CELSIUS	GAS
250	120	$\frac{1}{2}$
275	140	1
300	150	2
325	160	3
350	180	4
375	190	5
400	200	6
425	220	7
450	230	8
475	240	9
500	260	10

the perfect ending

Sweeten freshly brewed coffee to taste.
Pour over sprigs of fresh verbena or mint.
Steep for 2 minutes or to taste.
Strain, discard the herbs, and let the
coffee cool to room temperature.
Pour over ice.

For caffè corretto, add a shot
of whiskey to each serving.